Cross-Country Skiing for Everyone

Jules Older

Photography by Effin Older

STACKPOLE
BOOKS

Published by
STACKPOLE BOOKS
5067 Ritter Road
Mechanicsburg, PA 17055
www.stackpolebooks.com

Printed in the United States of America

10 9 8 7 6 5 4 3 2 1

First edition

Library of Congress Cataloging-in-Publication Data

Older, Jules
Cross-country skiing for everyone/Jules Older.—1st ed.
p. cm.
Includes bibliographical references (p.).
ISBN 0-8117-2708-4
1. Cross-country skiing I. Title.
GV855.3.053 1998
796.93'2—dc21 98-12789

CIP

DEDICATION

This book is dedicated to the memory of one of its contributors, Allan Bard, "The Great Bardini."

Just as I was getting ready to send the final draft to the publisher, another contributor, Jonathan Wiesel, called to say that Allan had been killed in a climbing accident at Jackson Hole. Not Allan! He was as careful as he was skilled, the kind of skier to whom you'd gladly entrust your life. He'd been a backcountry guide plus alpine and nordic instructor for more than a quarter century and a veteran of ten major ski expeditions from the North Pole to New Zealand. He lived, skied, and guided from his home at the foot of the Eastern Sierra until July 5, 1997. Then, while guiding in the Grand Tetons, he slipped on an unexpected piece of ice and fell more than 100 feet to his death. He was forty-five years old. He'll be sorely missed by all who knew him.

Hey—be careful out there!

Allan Bard

CONTENTS

ACKNOWLEDGMENTS

I owe a great debt of thanks to the many contributors to this book. They are among North America's leading experts on cross-country skiing and outdoor adventure. *Merci beaucoup,* Jean Arthur, Allan Bard, John Brodhead, John Caldwell, Kate Carter, Jim Chase, John Dostal, Jane Emanuelson, Ron Ferra, Steve Gaskill, David Goodman, George Hall, Mark Lichtenstein, Mike Miller, Pepa Miloucheva, John Morton, Isa Oehry, Brian Powell, Suzanne Roy, Phil Savignano, Tony Scheier, John Smith, John Tidd, Mike Tuggy, Katherine Ward, and Bob Woodward. And a special thanks to my two main readers, Jonathan Wiesel and the editor *sans merci,* Effin Older, who also shot the photos.

Thanks, too, to the folks at Stackpole, especially Mark Allison, who made this project such a smooth operation from beginning to end.

A Note from the Author to the Person Reading This Standing Up at the Bookstore

I've read many a book while standing up at the bookstore. It's the best way of finding out whether a book is worth buying. Let me help you along. This is not a book for racers, for experts, for techno-weenies. It is for folks who are either thinking of trying cross-country skiing or who have tried it and want to know more before making a commitment to the sport. (Something like reading standing up before making a commitment to a book.)

A couple of things differentiate this book from others like it. It's among the very few that make sense of major changes in ski design, and it looks at recent major changes in ski waxes, both of which could save you money and prevent mistakes when you're buying gear.

But what really distinguishes this book from so many others is that it's designed for normal human beings, not superathletes, not college competitors, not iron jocks with the time and inclination to do two hundred one-armed push-ups and run up and down mountains to get an edge on the competition. It's for plain folks who want to have fun outside in winter. If you're one of them, it will take you where you want to go.

And it will do one more thing: It will serve as an antidote to the purists who would make a simple, easy-to-learn, easy-to-enjoy sport as complicated as rocket science, leading to unnecessary pain, failure, and self-doubt. Where there's a choice between a hard way and an easy way, this book goes for the easy way. Where there's a choice between the recreationist's way and the racer's way, it opts for the recreationist. Where there's a choice between the fun way and the "right" way—hey, aside from getting to the post office after a snowfall, the whole point of cross-country skiing is to have fun.

You seem to be, shall we say, warming to this subject, Jules.

Yeah, fair enough. Purism is a pet peeve.

Before we move on, would you care to explicate?

Let me give you an example from alpine skiing. (I'll give you one from cross-country in the chapter on striding.) The protagonist of my story is Bill. Bill is the instructor's instructor. Bill is such a great skier and teacher that he goes around North America giving clinics for the best instructors at the continent's best ski schools. Bill is the Zen maven of ski instruction.

It's the second day of a two-day clinic. Bill has gathered all the hotshot instructors around him to demonstrate some fine point or other, when all of a sudden he says, "See that woman skiing by herself? What's wrong with her technique?"

The students, all eager to be the smartest, quickly unleash a litany of faults. "She's too far forward." "Has a residual stem." "Plants her poles too gingerly." And so forth.

Bill turns to them and shakes his head. "What you're looking at is someone skiing in control. There's a smile on her face. She's getting down what's for her a challenging slope without terror or awkwardness. She's having fun. Ladies and gentlemen, there is nothing wrong with her technique."

As Allan Bard, a.k.a. "The Great Bardini," said, "There is not one right way. All forms of skiing are worthy and they complement each other. The more one knows about sliding on snow, the better it goes. We can borrow bits and pieces of technique and skill from all aspects of skiing without getting wrapped up in dogma and structure. We have the freedom to just do it!"

The kind of cross-country skiing that this book deals with is about pleasure, not perfection. Enjoy.

1

Beauty and the Best

Cross-country skiing is one of those rarest of human activities in which you have prodigious quantities of fun, clear your head of cobwebs, do your body a major favor, and experience all this—the fun, the clarity, the self-improvement—in an extraordinarily beautiful setting. For what else on earth looks so breathtakingly beautiful as a glistening coverlet of untracked snow? The lightly falling flakes, the transformed shapes of fir and pine, the frail white-on-white patterns of bird and squirrel tracks—their combined effect is an almost dizzying beauty. Add to that the smell of balsam, the tingle of crisp air, and the sound of . . . nothing at all. Until you stand stock-still in winter woods, you don't really know the sounds of silence.

When you break that silence, when you plant your poles and push off, the still, cold air isn't rattled by the noise of engines or the clamor of lift lines. Even in full flight, the only sounds you hear are the hiss of skis, the steady in and out of your own breathing, and the rhythmic *thump, thump, thump* of your heart.

Is this just too good to be true? It must cost a fortune. Maybe you need to be a superjock. Is it just for the young, the male, the northern-born, the something other than you?

The collective answer is no. In the 1970s someone came up with the phrase, "If you can walk, you can cross-country ski." That isn't quite true, but it's not far off the mark. Cross-country skiing is the winter sport for anyone with enough balance to ride a bike, enough muscle to climb a flight of stairs. It's for anyone as old as 2, as young as 111. It's available to anyone with occasional access to 6 or more inches of snow.

And that age range of 2 to 111 isn't something I invented. It's the skiing life of one Herman "Jackrabbit" Smith-Johannsen. Jackrabbit first donned skis at the age of 2 in his native Norway. He continued to ski, cut trails, and enter races in his adopted Canada until well past his hundredth birthday. He was on skis until five days before he died in his 111th year. By 1987, when he died at nearly age 112, he had spent well over a century on skis. One obituary read, "He believed in a simple, vigorous life, but he was no crabbed ascetic. He was a renowned story-teller, smoked and drank, and, in his 80s as a speaker at ski banquets, would astound the audience by walking on his hands along the head table." Though a single case does not a theory prove, Jackrabbit Johannsen's vigor and longevity certainly point to the healthfulness of cross-country skiing.

A sport that engages upper and lower body at every step has to be good for you. Especially when it's low-impact, and since skiing has less impact than walking and much less than running, it doesn't jar your joints at every step. On top of that, within a few minutes of getting off the level and striding uphill, you've entered an aerobic challenge greater and far more rewarding than any treadmill.

Unlike downhill skiing, cross-country allows you to climb hills without digging in your edges and walking like a duck. The first time you successfully ski uphill, it feels like a small miracle. You've been striding across a field, and as you start up a long slope, you discover that if you just keep going—keep doing what you've been doing—you continue making forward progress. Up, down, or on the level, cross-country skis take you where you want to go.

Along with some 4 million Americans and nearly 3 million Canadians, your destination may be one of six hundred cross-country skiing areas from the wilds of Newfoundland to the mountains of California. Your companions may be a Connecticut family skiing together, then picnicking together on the tailgate of their Volvo station wagon. They may be a French-speaking team of Quebec racers with flat stomachs and fire in their eyes. They may be a fifty-ish couple from Vermont, an Alberta grandmother celebrating her seventy-fifth birthday, or members of a New Jersey social club who have discovered cross-country skiing is a pastime they can enjoy together. They may be a giggling gaggle of schoolkids on a winter outing, determined to leave the teachers in their powdery dust. Later, as you share hot chocolate with your trailmates in the warming hut, the adults sit around the woodstove and discuss trail conditions, bemoan or exult in the amount of snow back home, and ask the kids traditional Dumb Adult Questions: "So. What grade are you in?"

On and off skis, cross-country skiing covers a multitude of pleasures. Let me tempt you with some examples.

During my first ten years on cross-country skis, I lived in New York City and spent every Christmas with family in Brownington, Vermont. I spotted a pair of Finnish-made wooden skis at Herman's, bought them for $25, figured out how to strap the things to my work boots, read a Swix pamphlet on how to wax them, and commenced skiing across the fields and through the woods of Brownington. During that decade, from 1962 to 1972, I never saw another skier, either live or on film; I guess that defines "self-taught."

Since then, I've skied with happy crowds in Ottawa during the Canadian capital's Winterlude festival, off the highest peak in Newfoundland, in a saddle high in the Sierras of Nevada, in the shadow of the Ruby Mountains of Colorado, and with dozens of African-Americans at the Black Summit in Utah. I've skied across Lake Louise and raced a team of huskies over a frozen lake in Maine. Once, during a rare snowfall, I skied through the streets of Dunedin, New Zealand, grinning gleefully at the startled citizens. I've skied on prepared tracks, across snow-covered golf courses, amidst rock and scrub in unsuccessful pursuit of a herd of caribou, through thorny puckerbrush on Vermont's Catamount Trail, and along the gently curving streets of a New Hampshire condo development. I've also skied across a snow-covered lava field in the frozen interior of Iceland, pulled at frightening speed behind an $80,000 Nissan Patrol (Fig. 2) equipped with fat studded tires, cellular phone, CB radio, two state-of-the-art locator systems, altimeter, clinometer, inflatable jack, and a power winch.

But for the most part, I ski from the back door of my home in Vermont's Northeast Kingdom. My wife, Effin, and I don boots and jump on our skis most days of winter, usually in the early afternoon. It's an hour-long ounce of prevention against cabin fever, repetitive strain injury, and computer madness.

Despite all these years on boards, I am not a gonzo skier, not a racer, not a fearless risk taker. The truth is, I still love to silently move through snowy field and forest.

Over the years I've come to realize how greatly skiing has enhanced my appreciation of winter. Rather than groan about shoveling driveways and

Fig. 2

getting the car stuck in snowbanks, I look at snow as an invitation to play. And though my snow play takes many other forms—alpine skiing, snowboarding, winter hikes, and building snowmen—cross-country skiing constitutes my most constant, enduring winter activity. I'm stronger, happier, and almost certainly saner because of it. Skiing has given me what backcountry guide Allan Bard called "a quiet mind and satisfied soul."

Fig. 3

A Winter's Diary: September 25

Too Early. In the midst of autumn, with the leaves just reaching their personal best in fall colors, we get a three-minute snow shower in Brownington, Vermont.

Too early! I'm still biking! Get hold of yourself till November!

Here is Kate Carter, editor of *Vermont Sports Today*, on the pleasures of cross-country skiing: "The feeling of gliding is what I love most about cross-country skiing. Gliding across a long, flat stretch, keeping my momentum going with long, relaxed strides and easy double-poling is sensational. Even more thrilling is gliding at high speeds downhill, mastering the forces of gravity while unleashing the flow of adrenaline. Most exhilarating, however, is the sensation of gliding uphill, actually defying gravity and skiing up hills as if they were flat.

"I know I am skiing well, that I have gone beyond shuffling, when I am gliding up a hill. It doesn't happen often, but once in a while everything comes together—a fresh dusting of powder, the right wax, proficient technique, intuitive balance—and not even gravity can hold me back."

If the sport sounds appealing, this book's for you. It tells you what you need to own and what you don't, what you should buy and what you can do without. It will help you choose the skis, boots, bindings, and poles that will bring you the greatest pleasure. It teaches you how to ski on the level, uphill and downhill, in groomed tracks, and through untracked powder. It instructs you how to ski safely, efficiently, and powerfully. It explains striding, skating, and telemarking. It offers advice on ski and environmental etiquette. It tells you how to take care of your equipment, how to wax, and whether to wax.

This book will teach you the difference between ski touring and bushwhacking, skating and striding, waxing and not waxing. It will describe places to ski you've always dreamed about and suggest places you never thought of.

This book will take you where you want to go.

2

What Is Cross-Country Skiing?

I want to be sure that when we speak of cross-country skiing, we're talking about the same thing. So let us define our terms. *Skiing* is moving over snow with runners on your feet that let you glide. *Cross-country skiing* is moving over snow with runners on your feet that let you glide and also let you comfortably walk and shuffle, stride or skate, ascend as well as descend hills.

The common characteristic of all cross-country skiing is that your heel is free, unattached to the ski. It's that free heel that allows you to comfortably walk, shuffle, stride, skate, and climb.

In alpine skiing—another sport I love—the heel is held down, virtually glued to the ski by the binding. This may seem an insignificant difference, but on snow it's of major consequence. When your heel is stuck firmly to the ski, you gain an enormous amount of control by using your whole foot to power the ski through turns. With heel down and edges sharp, you can carve beautiful arcs down the steepest mountain.

That's a difficult, though not impossible, trick on cross-country skis. Paul Parker described it this way in his book, *Free-Heel Skiing*: "Downhill skiing on skinny skis can be like driving a '55 Ford with bald tires—skiddy, unsure, and imprecise. Alpine skiing is at the other end of the spectrum: fast, crisp, and exact—more like driving a Porsche."

So why not go for the Porsche? Why not lock the heels in for cross-country? Because you lose so much flexibility. On downhill skis, simple walking is hard work; climbing is hard, awkward, and inefficient. Unfun.

But cross-country skiing is all-terrain skiing. With free heels and lightweight skis, boots, and bindings, you can snake through a maple grove, whip along a prepared track, fly across a frozen lake with the wind at your back, or ski the Alps from peak to peak. Cross-country—also called *ski touring, nordic skiing,* or *skinny skiing*—takes you where you want to go.

And it does so with admirable simplicity—one person on a pair of skis, operating under his own power, enjoying glide, exercise, and the outside world in winter.

There are many kinds of skiing, and a fair number come under the same rubric. Ski jumping, for instance, is as different from cross-country skiing as you could imagine—jumpers don't stride through woods in their sport, we don't leap off high towers in ours—but both are categorized as nordic sports. So are telemarking and that strange combination known as the biathlon, in which you ski and shoot, ski and shoot, ski and shoot. Alpine sports are no less complex. They include slalom, giant slalom, downhill racing, freestyle, speed skiing, ballet, bump competitions, and snowboarding.

The difference is in the heel. If the heel is free, it's a nordic sport; if it's clamped firmly to the ski, it's alpine. That simple distinction will make things much clearer the next time you watch the Winter Olympics.

The heel binding isn't the only distinction between alpine and nordic skiing, however. Here's how the sports stack up:

- In the United States, more than 9 million people identify themselves as alpine (downhill) skiers and more than 2 million call themselves snowboarders. Nearly 3.5 million say they're nordic (cross-country) skiers.
- Despite the disparity, the number of ski areas for each sport is nearly identical. In 1997 the United States supported about five hundred alpine areas and five hundred cross-country areas. Why? In part, because it's far less expensive to build a nordic area than an alpine area. Trails through the woods and a warming hut are a real bargain compared with high-speed, detachable, sextuple chairlifts and ever more massive base lodges.
- In addition, there are countless miles of park and parking lot, logging road and snowbound street, great outdoors and small backyards that are used by nordic skiers every day of every winter. They're used without ski patrols, public toilets, or entry fees.
- The median age of the alpine skier is twenty-five to thirty-four; the nordic skier, thirty-five to forty-four. And both groups are older than snowboarders, whose median age is twelve to seventeen.
- The sexes break down differently as well. Snowboarders are 73 percent male; alpiners, 61 percent; and nordic skiers, 51 percent. In some years, female nordic skiers slightly outnumber males.

Jean Arthur is one helluva downhill skier. She rips, she roars, she races. But recently, she's been spending more and more time on cross-country skis. I asked, "How come?" Here's her answer:

"You asked why I became a nordic skier after having spent the better part of three decades with locked-down heels. I need to think on this as I slip quietly past a colt and his mother in the pasture next to my hometown ski tracks. He barely notices me and instead seems fascinated by the steam he blows from his youthful nostrils.

"You asked why I like to ski hard for my evening jaunt, without noisy kids, and line-cutting tourists. It's hard to think up a good answer while I'm skiing under a full moon with stars so bright that I don't need a headlamp.

"You asked why I traded in cold, hard plastic boots for cozy leather ones. Since my feet (and hands and heart) are still quite warm from today's 15k, I can tell you that there's nothing quite like the scrunching sound of cowhide against laces with each stride.

"Guess I can't answer you other than to say that I'll think about it tomorrow when I ski once again."

VARIETIES OF CROSS-COUNTRY EQUIPMENT

Racing skis are light, fast, and so narrow they're positively anorexic. Mountaineering skis have steel edges and are solid enough to withstand close encounters with trees. Telemark skis have a shape and structure of their own. Skating skis have a different bottom contour than striding skis, and waxless skis have a different bottom composition than waxable skis. Short skis look like, but aren't, a junior model of full-size skis. Fat skis are a recent trend that presents a linguistic dilemma in a sport frequently referred to as "skinny skiing." The next chapter looks at the differences in detail and, more important, will help you choose the skis that best fit your needs—and your expense account.

Fig. 4 *Different types of skis*

It's not just the skis that differ with the task at foot. Within cross-country, you can choose from a great number of boots, bindings, even poles, also covered in the next chapter.

As for clothes, compare the Lycra-clad Olympic racer with the tweed-knickered weekend strider; the contrast could hardly be greater. Though clothing distinctions are important—if you go ski mountaineering dressed in racing gear, you could freeze to death—for most new skiers, they're far from day-to-day reality. Cross-country skiing requires a minimum of equipment, and though you can continue learning new tricks and polishing old skills for your entire life, you can move and glide and have fun long before your first morning on skis is over. The good times begin almost immediately.

CLASSIC SKIING

Let's get on with our definitions, starting with classic skiing, or striding. *Classic skiing* means pushing (which skiers call "kicking") down and back with one ski in order to drive the other ski forward. At its heart is the diagonal stride, so named because when you kick with your left foot, you pole with your right arm, forming a diagonal line of working muscles.

Skating on skis, on the other hand, is much like skating on ice skates. In both sports, you start your glide by pointing blade or ski outward and pushing off a moving foot. In classic skiing, your skis move straight ahead; in skating, they are always moving away from each other. Since only one ski touches the snow at a time, you progress between them, rather than find yourself doing the split.

Fig. 5 *Striding (left) and skating (right)*

NORDIC DOWNHILL AND TELEMARKING

A third style of free-heel skiing is nordic downhill, whose best-known maneuver is the telemark turn, a long, graceful turn with one leg bent behind the other. You point the forward ski in the direction you want to turn and, as you sink into a genuflect, push the tip of the rear ski into the leading ski's side. Once you get the hang of it, you can cut elegant curves all the way down a mountainside.

The reason downhill free-heel skiing is called nordic downhill instead of telemarking is because the telemark turn is only one of the techniques used by downhillers. Others are wedge turns, parallel turns, step turns, and skating turns.

Fig. 6 *Telemarkers*

Ron Farra, a freelance writer, nordic ski enthusiast, cochairman of the Nordic Committee for the North American Ski Journalist Association, and editor of the *Nordic Newsletter* of the New York State Ski Racing Association, has this to say about nordic skiing:

"Imagine cross-country skiing with an archery bow and a quiver full of arrows over your shoulder, a .22-caliber rifle on your back, or a topo map in front of your chest. Imagine what it would be like to fly off a ski jump, to make beautiful telemark turns in the pristine snow of the backcountry, or to be pulled by your dog across a snow-covered lake on cross-country skis. These are all real sports, and all are part of the nordic experience.

"If you enjoy hunting or target shooting, you might try biathlon, the sport of cross-country skiing and rifle marksmanship. Biathlon has become a year-round activity enjoyed by runners in the nonsnow months. Another popular shooting activity has been joined with cross-country skiing to create the new sport of ski archery. As in biathlon, archers ski one or two miles before shooting at targets. With their pulses racing, skiers steady their bodies, take aim, and shoot their arrows before continuing to the next station or to the finish line.

"Good map-reading skills and quick decision making are essential qualities for ski orienteering. Cleverness is usually more important than skiing ability, as orienteerers study their maps to decide on the best route to the control points and to the finish line.

"Dogs that love to pull are easily harnessed for pulling their masters on skis. Called *skijoring,* this winter activity can be a simple recreational adventure with your canine pet or an exciting race at a regional or national sled-dog competition.

"You can take lessons in ski jumping at specialized facilities throughout the snowbelt. More girls and women are taking up this nordic sport since the U.S. Ski Association approved a competitive female classification. At the first ever ski jump competition exclusively for women, at Rumford, Maine, an eighteen-year-old broke the old hill record held by a male. Both men and women also compete in an Olympic sport joining ski jumping and cross-country skiing, called *nordic combined.*

"Each of these activities has a group of enthusiastic supporters who are always ready to encourage and assist those interested in trying a new winter sport. To learn more, contact one or more of the following:"

New England School of Archery, 109 School St., Concord, NH 03301, (803) 224-5768.

U.S. Biathlon Association, Camp Johnson, Colchester, VT 05446, (802) 864-1316.

Orienteering North America, 23 Fayette St., Cambridge, MA 02139, (617) 868-7416.

Ski Jump Camps, c/o Kodak Park, Lake Placid, NY 12946, (800) 463-6235.

U.S. Telemark Ski Association, 2552 E. 1700 S., Salt Lake City, UT 84108, (801) 582-8621.

Skijoring, c/o Roy Smith, 2626 Route 29, Johnstown, NY 12095, (518) 581-8103.

Professional Ski Instructors of America, 1-A Lincoln Ave., Albany, NY 12205, (518) 452-6095.

WAXED AND WAXLESS SKIS

Striding, skating, and telemarking require different skis for maximum efficiency and fun, which leads us to the next distinction, waxed and waxless skis.

Classic skiing feels like a small miracle: Your skis glide and grip, and they seem to know when to do which. But like many miracles, this one can be accounted for in earthly terms. To understand it, let's return to that diagonal stride.

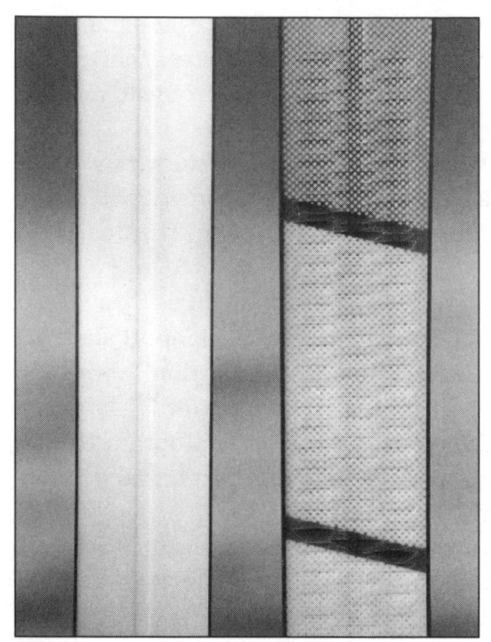

Fig. 7 *Ski bases, waxed (left) and waxless (right)*

While the left foot is kicking, the right is gliding. Kicking requires grip, or purchase, while gliding needs slide. Yet one set of skis does both. The question is, how? The answer is, through two neat tricks.

The first is built into the ski in the form of camber. Place a ski, base down, on a table. Put your eye at table height, and you'll see that ski meets table at two points—near the tip (the front) and near the tail (the rear end). The space in between is the *camber*, the high arc built into almost every ski (Fig. 8). The parts of the ski touching the table make up the *glide zone*, the ski's running surface. The part in the air, the arc, is for grip.

Here's how it works in a waxed ski. The base of the arc contains the *kick zone*, which contacts the snow when you're pushing down for a kick. The entire ski base is waxed, but the kick zone takes a different kind of wax than the glide zone. Glide wax is designed to reduce friction, to make for a long, smooth glide over the snow. The kick zone uses grip wax, which skiers call kick wax, which increases friction for a strong push-off between glides. By applying wax of the right sort—which changes with temperature and snow conditions—you create a surface that has just the right grip when stationary

Fig. 8 *Camber*

but plenty of glide when moving. That lets you kick and glide, and it also lets you ski uphill. As the hill's incline slows you down, the bottoms get grippier. No wonder it feels like a miracle.

There are a few drawbacks to waxing, however. It takes practice, and it takes time. If conditions change in the middle of the day or the middle of a race, you have to stop and rewax. And it doesn't work well in marginal conditions, particularly when the snow is right around the freezing point. This may mean so little grip that your legs spin in place or so much grip that the bottoms of your skis pick up bigger and bigger balls of snow, until you look like you're skiing on volleyballs. When you see competitors stopping in the middle of the race and fiddling with the bottoms of their skis, they're desperately searching for the right wax for the changing conditions.

That's why waxless skis were invented. Instead of a layer of wax, they rely on a pattern pressed into the ski base or, in a brief and largely unsuccessful experiment, on chemical compounds injected into the base. The patterns more or less resemble fish scales. In marginal conditions, they beat the heck out of wax. But waxless bases have drawbacks as well. Under most conditions, they don't glide as well as properly applied wax. In a silent sport, they tend to be a bit noisy, and they're hated by purists.

I used to be a bit of a wax purist. I tried waxless skis shortly after they were introduced and found them slow, loud, and unfun. I vowed never to use them again. But ten years later, for an expedition into the mountains of Newfoundland, I picked up a pair anyway and discovered what a difference a decade makes. The new skis, Fischer Touring Crowns, were quieter, faster, and infinitely more fun than those I had used earlier. They were also the lightest and most versatile touring skis I'd ever tried, and they handled rapidly changing conditions with aplomb. I brought the skis home and haven't used waxed skis since.

SKIING AT SKI AREAS

Another distinction in cross-country skiing is between ski touring and ski-area skiing. When you've spent a day touring through the woods on logging roads, there's no hot chocolate machine, no porcelain toilets, no blazing fireplace waiting for you at the warming hut. There's no warming hut. There's also no trail fee. But the biggest difference is that there's no trail grooming, which is the main thing you're buying with your trail fee.

Trail grooming means setting parallel tracks for classic skiers and a smooth, broad snow road for skaters. A good ski area will groom trails nightly and sometimes during the day as well. The usually modest sum you pay pretty much guarantees a well-maintained surface designed specifically for skiing. The warming hut is thrown in free.

Winter's Diary: October 4

Gimme a Break! By noon the morning rain has turned to sleet. By 1:30 the sleet has turned to snow. Unlike last month's flurry, this time it's for real. At 4:00, the thermometer squats on 32 and the snow lays 4 inches deep on the car, on the street, on the ground. Sophie, the half husky, loves it, but I don't. I've got a three-day mountain bike trip coming up next weekend, and the thought of slogging through the back roads of Craftsbury in snow and slush does not amuse me even a little. Gimme a break, will ya? Just hold the snow until, say, Thanksgiving.

The other type of ski-area skiing is nordic downhill, which consists of telemarking and other descent turns, often pursued at alpine ski resorts. Here, the trails are more vertical than horizontal, the warming hut is a mega–base lodge, and though you're less likely to see a moose in the trail, you're much more likely to encounter something far more frightening—a snowboarder.

Ski touring is skiing away from ski areas. But cross-country ski areas are called touring centers. So to tour, stay out of touring centers. Let us resolve this paradox by renaming ski touring "off-trail skiing." The idea is that you're creating your own tracks, not following those laid down by a grooming machine. We'll call that "set-track skiing."

BACKCOUNTRY SKIING

Backcountry skiing is another story—actually, several stories. The roughest form is ski mountaineering, which you do with steel-edged skis and heavy boots. Ski mountaineers like narrow trails and windblown peaks; they trek the length of the Alps and the peaks of the Rockies.

Right behind mountaineering on the roughness index is bushwhacking, the art of making your own trails through the snow-covered wilderness. Next down the list is ungroomed trail skiing. The trails can range from an unplowed highway (Vermont's Route 108 from Stowe to Smugglers' Notch is a favorite) to an old miner's trail (Crested Butte, Colorado, is laced with them) to a logging road (Maine and Newfoundland have logging roads aplenty). If there's one person in your party who's stronger, keener, and younger than the rest, send her ahead to break trail. If not, trade off every so often; as with so much of life, it's considerably harder to lead than to follow.

Finally, we come to skiing on snowmobile trails. They're groomed for machines, not skis, but compared with bushwhacking, snowmobile trails are sheer luxury. They can also be dangerous. Ways to minimize this danger are discussed in chapter 7.

Fig. 9 *Ski trails by Vermont Sugarhouse*

3

Ski Gear

Buying ski gear is something like buying a car. By the time you consider all the options, you're exhausted. This chapter is designed to reduce shopping fatigue while helping you find the right equipment for your needs.

In a world where almost nothing is cheap, cross-country skiing is a genuine bargain. Skis are much cheaper than golf clubs. Trail fees are a tiny fraction of tennis court fees. You needn't buy oxygen as in diving, or padding as in hockey. And you can fully outfit yourself for cross-country skiing for less than the price of a decent pair of downhill ski *bindings*. Here are the stats: In 1995 the average alpine skier spent $281 on skis; the average skinny skier, $115. For boots, $230 versus $91. Bindings, $128 versus $38.

SKI TYPES

So many skis, so many choices! If you're new to the sport, that's what you're going to think the first time you enter a ski shop. But reading this chapter before shopping will make your decisions easier.

Let's start with the process of elimination. Walk right on by the racks of alpine skis; that eliminates two-thirds of the merchandise. Then, unless you're looking for telemark skis, ones you'd use primarily on downhills and at alpine resorts, walk by those too.

Next, think about a simple ratio: How much skiing will you do in set tracks at cross-country areas compared with backcountry skiing along snowmobile trails or through virgin snow? If the answer is 8:1 or higher, go for skis designed for tracks. They're thinner, faster, and weigh less than their backcountry cousins. If the ratio is the opposite, go for the backcountry skis. They're slower but less likely to break in the great outdoors. If your use ratio is more like 5:5, go for an in-between ski, sometimes called a combi or cross-touring ski, designed for use in and out of tracks. And if you're intending to race, buy racing skis (and a racing book to supplement this one).

Racing skis run from about 43 to 45 millimeters wide, touring skis about 46 to 47 millimeters, and backcountry skis start around 50 millimeters, and grow wider each year. Nordic downhill/telemark skis usually run 55 millimeters or wider and have steel edges. Those edges are great for cutting quick turns down icy steeps, but they also cut glide time so they're much slower on the flats. Ski maven Jonathan Wiesel cautions, "Stores consistently sell overkill—excessively heavy everything. Partly that's ignorance, partly it's an assumption that width connotes stability. If people take instruction, they can do just fine (especially on groomed trails) without that extra weight, sweat, and irritation."

Fig. 10 *Ski tops*

Fig. 11
Ski bottoms (left to right): no edge, partial edge, full edge

Now, answer honestly: Are you a person who values perfection over convenience? Do you like to tinker? Will you make the time for preski preparation? If your answer is yes, then buy skis with waxable bases and pick up a selection of waxes, some wax remover, a scraper, and a special cork for rubbing the wax in. Otherwise, buy a waxless model. A word of caution, though: *Waxless* refers only to kick wax; all skis should be glide waxed, but only two or three times a season.

Before you grab a pair off the rack, there's still another choice to make: Will you be mainly skating or striding? Here it helps if you've already tried both. We'll come to that shortly. But before we do, there's one last choice.

Until 1992 ski choices were limited to waxed or waxless, striding or skating, racing or touring, in-track or backcountry. Then things got more complicated. Fischer announced a new category of skis, which they dubbed the Revolution. The Revolution was lighter, more maneuverable, and easier to learn on than other skis, and it was barely half their length. In a sport where the standard way to pick the correct length was to reach up as high as you could and buy the ski that tickled your palm, Fischer now had a one-size-fits-all model that convention would say shouldn't fit anyone but a midget. For purists, this defined size shock. And what was worse, the darned things worked. Gonzo ski writer Bob Woodward reported, "The Revolutions are coming and boy are they fun."

Bob Woodward has been photographing and writing about cross-country skiing for more than twenty-five years. Since he first reported on short skis, he's had many a chance to reflect on his early enthusiasm. Here's what he thinks today:

"From the first time I tried the Revolutions, I knew that cross-country ski technology had finally taken a turn for the better. It wasn't so much that the single size short skis made us ski better, it was that we were having a lot more fun. On the feet of experienced skiers, the Revolutions were a hoot. Over a three-day period, our group of adults with thick skiing résumés acted like kids on holiday after being cooped up for months. We held jumping contests, slalom races, ski ballet contests, all inspired by these short, easy-to-maneuver skis.

"Today the novelty has worn off. Though they're not for everyone, I still think shorties serve a purpose as the perfect skis for learning the skate technique, for learning the basics of turning, and to get a feeling of ski control.

"More significantly, short skis led us to midlength skis, and in my book the midlength skis—particularly the midlength generously fat skis like the Trak Bushwacker and the Karhu Catamount—are the cross-country skis to own today.

"Middies first took off in racing. Then Trak and Karhu introduced midlength touring skis that were wider at tip, tail, and waist than traditional touring skis. Now we had a wider, more stable ski that could turn because of ample sidecut and that was rock-solid stable.

"I have my old, general-purpose 215-centimeter touring skis up on the wall. In memory, those big monsters glided effortlessly but took the strength of seven Sly Stallones to get into a turn; they were about as maneuverable as a semi in a snowstorm. Now I plunk around on a pair of 190-centimeter midlength fat skis that glide well, turn like a dream, and offer a very stable platform. [They come up to the 6-foot, 4-inch Woodward's eyebrows, and he uses them mostly for out-of-track classic skiing.]

"The legacy of the Revolution skis is a rethinking and reenergizing of a sport whose ski technology, apart from racing, had been on hold for far too long."

Within a year, other companies had shorties on the market, notably, the Rossignol Tempo and the Peltonen Micro. Roof rack manufacturers started biting their nails; these new skis fit neatly in the trunk. By 1994 the Revolution was Fischer's top-selling ski, and John Sleuber, owner of Royal Gorge, the biggest cross-country skiing area in the United States, said, "I predict that within five years you won't be able to buy a long ski."

Sleuber was wrong about the ski but right about the trend. Shorter (though not nearly as short as the Revolution) is the way skis are going.

I've skied the Revolution, both skating and striding models. My regular skis are 210 centimeters long. My skate Revolutions are 147. My Revolution Controls, which are made for classic skiing, are 167.

So, having tried long and short, which do I think you should buy?

First, I suggest you try both before you buy either. Second, as a rule of thumb, if you're just learning to ski or planning to ski mostly in set tracks, I'd give the nod to the short skis, but not to the supershorts that Fischer originally introduced. Instead, go for a shortish ski, of which there are now many. Disregard this if you weigh more than 150 pounds. If you're over 150 and/or you're a backcountry type, long (and now fat) models will give you better support as well as more flotation over untracked powder or breakable crust. If you're on the cusp, I'd go for the long guys.

Here's the bottom line: For the most versatile skis you can buy, I recommend a waxless, full-length, classic fiberglass model that's wide enough for bushwhacking and narrow enough to fit in tracks. All the leading manufacturers, including Alpina, Fischer, Karhu, Madshus, Rossignol, and Trak, make them. These are skis that will pretty much take you wherever you want to go.

Why a classic ski over a skating ski? It's more adept at handling both jobs. You can skate on a classic ski more easily than you can stride on a skater.

If you can afford two sets of skis, I'd buy a combination boot and get the ski above plus a short skating ski.

Size and Flex

Assuming you decide on a traditional-length model, here's how to determine how long your skis should be. Hold your hand straight up above your head. A classic ski should come roughly to your wrist. A skating ski should come roughly to your forearm. "Roughly" because if you're not a racer, an inch or so in either direction won't matter, and because your weight is actually more important than your height. If you're a heavyweight, buy a ski that's higher than your wrist; if you're a flyweight, buy shorter. As the current trend is to shorter, wider skis, it's probably best to err in this direction. But if you've got it roughly right, that's good enough.

Without getting too technical about it, *flex* is how hard you have to push to flatten your skis against the resistance of the camber. Some would say that flex is at least as important as length in choosing a ski. A ski with soft flex is best for lightweight skiers; one with hard flex is best for heavyweights. Trouble is, most ski manufacturers don't publicize the flex characteristics of their various models, and if you're buying waxless, you'll probably have little choice anyway. That's why I so strongly urge you to try before you buy.

Once you've got all that settled, you can walk into the shop with head held high. Tell the clerk what kind of skiing you do and what sort of ski you're looking for. From there on, it's down to brands and prices.

Here's one caution, however, from Jim Chase, editor and publisher of *Cross Country Skier* magazine: "Based on the mistaken impression that what most cross-country skiers want to do is to simply walk on skis, there has been a proliferation of sliding snowshoes appearing on the ski shop racks—wide, short skis that don't glide much and sell cheaply. People are lured into the sport with promises of adventure and fun, and then saddled with inferior gear that makes the real enjoyment of cross-country skiing—glide—impossible."

BUYING USED SKIS

If you can't afford good stuff, you can wait for the end-of-season sale in spring or buy used. Find out when the local ski club is holding its annual swap meet and get there early in the day. Generally, avoid buying any bindings, skis, or boots more than two or three years old, and be sure to check that binding screws are tight, skis are straight, and boots aren't excessively worn. Then boldly step up and claim your bargain. It's better to buy high-quality gear that's been lightly used than low-quality gear that won't give much use.

If you're buying used skis, either privately or at a swap, don't take the skis if:

- There's little or no camber left. If the bottoms touch the ground from tip to tail, they're out of camber.
- They're warped or twisted. Sight down the skis from tip to tail. If you see a twist, put them back on the rack.
- The bottom is deeply gouged. Minor cracks can be easily filled, but if a gouge goes deep into the core of the ski, it could have soaked water where it's supposed to be dry. Check the sidewalls and tails as well. Water loves cracks.
- The top has filled-in screw holes all over the midsection. It's either had too many bindings or too many owners.
- It has three-pin bindings. Unless it's a telemark or backcountry ski, that probably means it's lived out its useful life.

Try, Then Buy

I'm a firm believer in trying before buying. For skis, boots, and bindings — even for the sport itself—I urge you to try before you buy. You may hate short skis. You may hate purple boots. You may hate cross-country skiing. No sport is for everyone, skiing included. And trying it is so easy.

If you live near a cross-country center, rent equipment there. Tell them the kind of skiing you most want to try and seek their advice on what gear to rent. If you don't live near a cross-country center, do exactly the same at your nearest ski shop, and get their advice on where to ski as well. A third alternative is to hook up with the outing club of a nearby college, find out who their skiers are, and seek their advice. Many clubs have rental or loaner skis on hand; if you show interest, they may let you try a few pairs.

One day a year, ski areas all over North America hold Ski Fest, a celebration of cross-country skiing designed to encourage first-timers to try the sport. The event includes free lessons, free equipment to demo, and sometimes free skiing. Ski Fest '97 was held on January 12, with 116 areas opening their ski schools to potential skiers. You could have joined the fun if you were in Alaska, Alberta, British Columbia, Ontario, or Quebec, or in California, Colorado, Connecticut, Idaho, Illinois, Maine, Massachusetts, Michigan, Minnesota, Montana, New Hampshire, New Jersey, New Mexico, New York, Oregon, Pennsylvania, Utah, Vermont, Washington, West Virginia, Wisconsin, or Wyoming. To find out where and when you can go in other years, contact Ski Fest, 259 Bolton Road, Winchester, New Hampshire 03470, (603) 239-8888, www.xcski.org/skifest.html.

BOOTS

In any kind of skiing, boots, not skis, are the most crucial piece of equipment you'll own. You can turn on mediocre skis if you're wearing good boots, but turning is hell on good skis and miserable boots. If you're caught between buying great skis and ho-hum boots or vice versa, put your main money into boots.

Fig. 12 *Boots*

In boots, fit is much more important than brand. Try them on in the store. Walk around in them. Squat, stretch, make a spectacle of yourself. Ignore the stares of other customers—you have to find how they fit your *moving* foot. If the boots hurt in the store, they'll be murder on the trail.

Too-tight boots are agonizing, and not just because they rub or pinch your feet. If your toes press against the front of the boot every time you stride or skate, they'll be black and blue before the day is out. If your toes are cramped, they're prime candidates for frostbite.

But too-loose and too-soft boots are nearly as bad. With no support, you'll tire easily. Your ankles may give way. And getting your skis to turn will feel like coming about in an ocean liner. Watch out for soft "noodle boots" if you're buying used equipment.

The best thing you can do for your boots and yourself is to avoid clomping around in them. Except for heavy-duty backcountry models, their soles are made of plastic that's not only subject to scratches and gouges but also dangerously slippery. It's important to clean your boots as soon as you take them off. This isn't for looks; clean boots are less likely than dirty ones to collect ice.

Cuffs

Some ski boots come with cuffs; some don't. The cuffs, or collars, serve two purposes. One is to keep deep snow out of your socks and ankles; the other—if the cuff has some built-in lateral support—is to make skating easier. Of course, cuffs add weight, and even a little extra weight about the ankles can be tiring on a long trip.

To save money or to use only in set tracks, get cuffless boots. To ski in snow more than a few inches deep, get cuffs. Or get both by buying a boot with removable cuffs. Most boot companies make them; ask to try on a combination boot.

BINDINGS

There used to be just one binding system: the 75-millimeter, three-pin system. The boot's sole extended out in front, where three holes in its bottom fit snugly into a plate with three protruding pins screwed to the ski. It worked well, but it had its problems. One was that the pins tended to wear down the holes until, pretty soon, nothing fit. Another was that the front-only contact gave precious little sideways (lateral) control over the ski, so turns usually involved holding your tongue—the one in your mouth—in just the right position.

Today, two other boot bindings have replaced the three-pin system for most purposes. The Salomon SNSX/Profil and the Alpina/Rottefella NNN II (NNN stands for New Nordic Norm) do away with the extended sole, the worn-out holes, and the pins. Instead, they have a raised platform that slides into grooves in the sole of the boot every time you lower your heel. This positive connection gives far greater sideways control than pins and holes. And most of the new bindings are step-ins; to start skiing, you line up the toe of your boot with the toepiece of the binding and step down. Click. That's all there is to it.

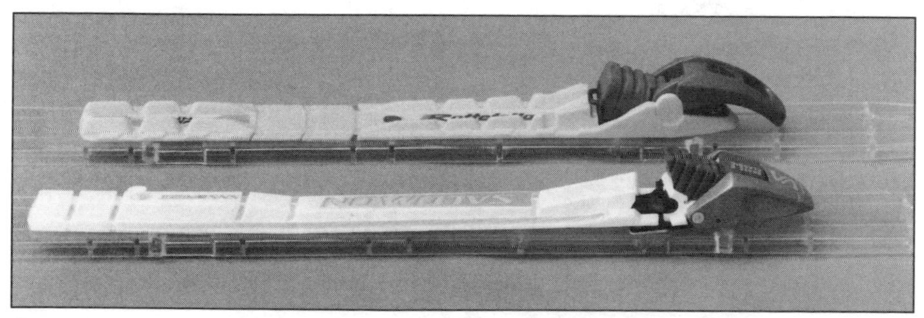

Fig. 13 *Bindings (front) Salomon SNS (back) NNN*

Should you buy Profil or NNN? Doesn't matter; both hold the toe firmly to the ski, allow freedom for the heel, and nicely catch the sole of the boot so that it doesn't slip over the side of the ski every time you set it down. One thing, though—if you own more than a single set of skis or if there are two or more skiers in the family, get one system and stick with it. That way your skis are interchangeable and you needn't swap boots every time you swap skis. Should you buy step-ins? Absolutely. Unless you can think of a pressing reason not to, always go for products that will save you from fiddling around in the snow with cold fingers.

Telemark skiing and heavy-duty ski trekking and mountaineering have their own bindings. Both use solid, somewhat heavier bindings that rely on three pins and a heel cable or a beefed up, backcountry Nordic Norm known as BKNNN. They're both designed for heavy boots and wide skis in serious terrain. For other conditions, however, they are overkill.

Fig. 14 *SNS (left) and NNN (right) bindings and boots*

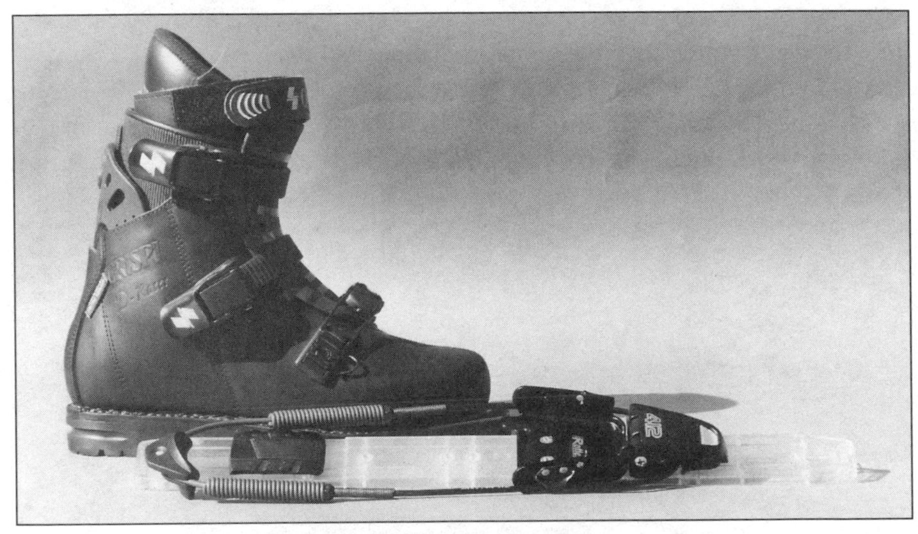

Fig. 15 *Telemark boots and binding*

Whatever binding you buy, you must buy the corresponding boot. There's no way to squeeze an NNN boot into a three-pin binding. Decide which boot-and-binding combination meets your needs, and buy them together.

POLES

In the old days, poles were poles. They were made of bamboo with straight leather handles, cost $10, and the only choice you had was length. Today poles are made of just about anything—fiberglass, aluminum, graphite, titanium, uranium, compressed moon dust. They come with straight handles, curved handles, handles that look like an ocarina or a kazoo. They cost anywhere from $12 to the price of a low-mileage Jaguar.

After deep scientific study, precise measurement, and objective analysis, I have reached the conclusion that poles are poles. My fiberglass Exels cost $12, and they've lasted ten years with no sign of wearing out and no replacement parts other than an occasional change of basket, which costs about two bucks.

But not all poles are the same size. Skaters usually use longer poles than striders—somewhere between chin and nose height for skaters versus shoulder height for striders. Don't think of this as a hard-and-fast rule; the fashion changes from year to year.

Whatever poles you buy, make sure they come with adjustable straps. Hands come in different sizes, as do gloves and mittens. You might also consider buying an extra pair of baskets, the doohickeys near the bottom of the

Fig. 16 *Pole baskets*

Winter's Diary: October 5

Awright, Awready. Look, I don't want to ski. I've got a cold. I've got work to do. There are leaves on the trees. And though frost has blackened the marigolds and morning glory, the parsley's still green by the front door and the brown-eyed Susans are smiling bravely in the garden. And it is October. Early October.

But it's no good. When I awake to a floodlit, blue-sky morning with 5 inches of new snow on the ground, I know this is going to be a ski day. I race through breakfast, find a turtleneck at the bottom of my drawer, search the attic for ski boots and a hat, and fairly dance out to the barn to get my skis. They're there, right behind the fishing gear, and what's more, they still have klister on their bottoms. By now, Effin and our neighbor, Marsha, are as ready as I am to get out in this unexpected snow, and Sophie, our half husky, can't believe her luck.

We slip into the skis at the door. Then, rather gingerly, we slide down the gentle slope into the field next door to see if we remember anything from last winter about how to make these things stop and go.

It all comes back: the power kick, the extra push from the pole, and best of all, the glide. It's that glide that puts cross-country skiing in a different league from snowshoeing and that gives it a double bonus—the tingle of modest speed and the pleasure of getting something for nothing. It's that bonus that makes skiers itch for snow. Even in early October.

We head across the road, up into the big field, and over the crest of the hill. There, to the east, lies Burke Mountain, framed by Mounts Hor and Pisgah. Snow covers the trees on the mountains, and the rolling meadows leading up to them are as white as a farmwife's sheets. Turn west and there's the top third of Jay Peak, its snow-covered trails sharply delineated in the clear morning air. Nearby, the green and gold and crimson of the maples at the field's edge stand out sharply against the white foreground and background.

Sophie loves all of it. So do Marsha and Effin. So do I.

Skiing under fall foliage at the beginning of October. Wonderful!

poles that keeps them from sinking into the snow (Fig. 16). If you're in the backcountry, a bigger basket handles soft snow better; in set tracks, a small, asymmetrical basket is more energy efficient. Try before you buy, and get the pole that pleases you most. Just don't waste too much time thinking about it.

GEAR TO AVOID

In everything except poles, there is something to avoid when buying ski gear: the low-end stuff. It's true, you don't need race-quality gear to enjoy skiing, but you do need equipment that functions smoothly, efficiently, and comfortably. If you've taken my advice to try before you buy, you'll have a pretty good idea that you're going to enjoy the sport you're gearing up for. So don't cap your enjoyment by buying equipment you're going to outgrow in a season or two. It's no bargain if your boots hurt, your skis don't glide, or your binding screws pull out in the middle of a cross-country trek. Go for the best you can afford; that's the real bargain.

Price aside, what distinguishes a good ski from one that's, at best, pretty good? One feature is a sintered base. Ski bases come in two types: extruded and sintered. Extruded bases are made from high-density polyethylene, which is cheap and reasonably durable. Sintered bases are made from ultra-high-molecular polyethylene, which is more expensive, considerably more durable, and holds wax much better. Sintered bases also give better glide, save energy, and increase enjoyment. It's worth paying extra for the sinter.

4

Clothes

Just for fun, let's start with what you don't need in the way of ski clothes. It's fun because if you're on a tight budget, you hardly have to spend anything. So here's what you don't need.

- Lycra. Those skin-tight, boldly colored Lycra suits are really designed for racers—they're sexy and aerodynamic, but they're not warm. If you aren't concerned about saving nanoseconds by lowering wind resistance, skip the Lycra.
- Knickers. Sure, the old-timers swear by them, but short pants and long socks do not a skier make.
- Ski gloves. Former U.S. team coach John Caldwell favors $2 garden gloves until things get really cold.
- Ski goggles. The right sunglasses will do just fine. I'll describe them below.
- Ski hat. Any hat that covers your ears will protect you from the cold.
- Ski parka. You can ski in a windbreaker, a sweater, or a shirt, depending on the weather.

What you do need is a considerably shorter list. Here it is:

- Wicking underwear, not cotton.
- Layers of clothing you can take on and off.

When you're dressing for cross-country skiing, you have two objectives and one requirement. The objectives are to keep warm and dry; the requirement is freedom of movement. The warmth is self-evident, the dryness may surprise you, and the freedom we'll talk about now.

STAYING FREE

Cross-country skiing is a sport of big movements. Your arms fling almost straight out, front and rear. Your legs stretch way behind you and, in skating, well to the side. You bend your knees and ankles, and in telemarking, bend them so far that your calf nearly rides on the snow. To do all this, wear clothes that won't constrict your movements. If it weren't for the weather, swimming shorts would be ideal. But given the weather, you should wear either skintight fabrics like Lycra or loose-fitting garments with lots of room in the shoulders, elbows, and knees. Think of oversize sweatshirt and sweatpants as a model. And they'd be fine if it weren't for the dryness factor.

STAYING DRY

When most people think of dressing for skiing, they think of keeping wetness—snow, rain, and hail—out. But a more serious problem is wetness from within: sweat. As soon as you get wet, from snow or sweat, you're going to get cold. Why? Because water conducts heat away from your body more than thirty times faster than air. That's called heat transport. It can kill you. Simply wearing more clothes is not the solution. You need to keep snow from coming in while letting sweat sneak out. It may sound impossible, but so did gliding and kicking on the same ski. And here, too, physics comes to the rescue, this time in the guise of *moisture vapor transport.* While a water-resistant outer shell keeps the elements out, multilayered synthetics move sweat up and away from your skin, leaving your body warm and dry, even when the outer fabrics are damp.

If you sweat a lot—you know who you are—buy a parka with a vented back or generous pit zips. Pit zips are underarm zippers that let your damp parts breathe freely. Right after Saran Wrap and digital watches, they're one of the great inventions of our time.

UNDERWEAR

In the old days, ski underwear could be described in one word: Duofold. Apart from a few knockoffs, Duofold's cotton-inner-layer, wool-outer-layer long johns were what everybody wore under their knickers. But cotton is far from ideal for skiers. When wet, it gives no warmth, and between snow and sweat, skiing is an activity that produces major quantities of wetness.

Then, in 1972, Italian scientists came up with new synthetic fibers capable of accomplishing things cotton never even dreamed of. Wet or dry, these test-tube creations protect better than cotton or wool. By enhancing moisture vapor transport, they wick perspiration away from the body to the outer garments, where it can evaporate without cooling you down like a plunge in an icy river.

The first of these materials was polypropylene, now called polyolefin. Then came treated polyesters. Then came bicomponent and tricomponent blends. Today, laboratory fabrics go by names like Aquator, BTU, Capilene,

Drylete, Fieldsensor, Hydrofil . . . and down through the alphabet to Qwick, Thermax, and Worsterlon. Whatever their make and model, synthetics wick better than cotton, wool, or silk.

Wicking is different from warmth. Ice fishermen need warmth. They spend a lot of time sitting around in cold places. Skiers need wicking, because we move around a lot, and perspire a lot, and because, as you now know, perspiration chills the body more than thirty times faster than cold air.

Ski underwear is now available with and without sleeves, ultrathin or extrathick, straight polyprop or blended fabric. If you own a couple of pairs, listen to the weather forecast and then choose the undergarment *du jour.*

How does the new stuff stack up with the old? How much is real improvement, and how much is hype? I assumed that hype outweighed improvement until I went cross-country skiing with a jock friend from Maine. After 10 kilometers of stop-start skiing, we returned to the warming hut, where I removed my sweater, turtleneck, and ten-year-old Duofold top, all of which were soaked with perspiration. She, who had matched me stride for stride the whole way, was dry as an iguana. "Cotton kills!" she said. "Get yourself some cold-weather gear!"

I did. I tested two weights of the new Duofold (now with Thermax replacing the cotton layer), Hot Chillys, and Patima Thermals. All were superior to my old long johns for dryness and warmth. All kept me comfortable. Hot Chillys were the jazziest, but the wool-Lycra blend was so itchy that they went to the Salvation Army. But this year I fingered a pair in a ski store and, to my great surprise, found that they'd gone from the scratchiest to the smoothest of the underwear. Except for the fact that Hot Chillys hasn't discovered the fly, they've become my fave first layer.

As for chill in intimate places, Jogbra, which did for athletic women what the jockstrap did for men, developed a wicking bra for sisters who ski. A number of other companies followed, leaving women with at least eight choices for avoiding chilly chests. In its January 1997 issue, *Vermont Sports Today* rated the bras for wicking, warmth, and comfort. Two clear winners appeared. For warmth but not wicking, the testers liked Goody's Fleece Bra (802-747-7299), declaring it was "like sleeping in flannel sheets." For top ranks in every category, they liked In Sport Elitist (800-652-5200). Champion (800-621-3682) and Moving Comfort (800-763-6000) also did well. Windproof underpants for men are also available from Louis Garneau.

OUTERWEAR

So much for underwear. In the old days, outerwear offered only two choices: goose down and junk. Goose down was warm, expensive, and made you look like the Michelin Man. Junk was anything else manufacturers threw into the linings of their bottom-of-the-line parkas. It was cheap, cold, and made you wish you'd taken up a warm-weather sport.

Down hasn't changed, but everything else has. Since the 1978 debut of Thinsulate, synthetics come with names from Aerozip to Ultrafibre. They run from high-loft (like down) to positively skinny. All exceed down at retaining warmth when wet, some reflect body warmth back to the skier, and most are still cheaper to buy than goose feathers.

All this is fine, but bear in mind that except in extreme conditions, you need *no* insulation in your parka. As long as you wear layers of clothing underneath it, a windproof shell is more than warm enough for most cross-country skiing.

Shell fabrics have changed, too. Increasingly, they're able to "breathe" (let sweat out) and resist penetration (keep snow out) at the same time. Each season, manufacturers come closer to the skiers' ideal—a fabric that is completely waterproof, windproof, breathable, soft, flexible, durable, and smashingly good looking. Today's test-tube fabrics come with names like Activent, Barrier, Cordura, Doeskin, ESP, all the way to Versatech and Zephyr.

If this weren't enough, outer garments from gloves to pants to parkas come equipped with built-in waterproofing. The best-known name in the field is Gore-Tex, thanks to Robert Gore's temper. In 1969, after a frustrating day spent fruitlessly trying to work Teflon into a fabric, he angrily grabbed a melting rod of the stuff and yanked it as hard as he could. Instead of breaking, it stretched. Gore and a host of competitors have been stretching similar products into waterproof, breathable clothing linings ever since. Some of the better known brands are Caltech, Entrant, H2ONO Storm, and of course, Gore-Tex.

Katherine Ward, operations manager of sportswear manufacturer Louis Garneau USA, cautions about coated clothing. Though most skiing apparel is machine washable, the garments that are coated for wind and water resistance are damaged by washing, she says. A bit more of the coating washes out with each washing, and it loses its protective qualities. What's more, many coatings restrict the garment's breathability.

A better alternative is to look for materials whose wind and water protection is built into their fabric. Here's how to recognize the difference: The label of coated clothing will say, "Such-and-such coating will protect against wind and water." Much better, look for one that says, "By construction, this material will protect against wind and water."

There is one other thing you should look for in cross-country skiwear. When you ski, you're creating a wind that comes right at you. So choose a parka that protects your front and ventilates your back. For maximum ventilation, buy one with a mesh back or a vented back.

All the above clothing items are grand advances in comfort and warmth, but none are my own personal favorite apparel. After a season of fifty-eight ski days and 20,000 travel miles, one undisputed winner emerged: The winner is (roll of drums) . . . the fleece pullover.

On all but the coldest days, the fleece has replaced sweaters, and on warm, windless days, it's eclipsed shells. What's more, my fleece has done duty as a pillow, backrest, seat cushion, and towel (not a great towel, but a towel nonetheless). And despite nearly constant use and abuse, I've worn it to some pretty classy restaurants without once getting the hairy eyeball from a maître d'.

Fleece pullovers are warm, wicking, and wicked comfortable. They machine wash and dry fast. They squash without wrinkling. They wear forever. And they're a lot cheaper than sweaters.

Nearly every company that makes ski clothes now makes a fleece pullover. Which one you buy largely depends on the features you like best. I like hand-size pockets, a high collar, and an adjustable neckline so I can ventilate when I'm hot and hunker down when I'm not. The one that lasted 20,000 miles is made by Land's End.

LAYERING

The most often-repeated advice to skiers is to layer their clothing. The space between layers traps warm air, and the process of insulation allows you to shed clothes when you're working, as in uphill skiing, and add them when you're not, such as when eating lunch at the summit.

Fig. 17

Think of ski clothing as a three-layered cake. Next to your body, wear wicking underwear. Above that, wear an insulating layer: a turtleneck, flannel shirt, or fleece. On the top, wear a weatherproof covering to keep out the elements.

In warm and windless weather, take off the outer layer. It's easiest if your parka crumples into its own zippered pack. On warm days, I wear a low turtleneck with a zippered neck so I can let heat escape without stripping to my underwear. When it gets really warm, I strip to my underwear.

When things get really cold, add extra layers, but be prepared to shed them when the activity of cross-country skiing warms your body against the weather. This sport produces great quantities of warmth as it exercises your body parts from the toes up.

FEET, HANDS, HEAD, AND NECK

Because of changes like the above, skiing is a warmer sport today than ever before. And this new warmth extends to the coldest-feeling parts of a skier's body: feet and fingers. Back when men were men and boots were cold, skiers used to wear two or three pairs of socks to keep their toes from turning to ice. Today, better boot design has made the layered look from the ankle down a relic of the old, cold past.

Today, most skiers wear one thin pair of ridgeless, seamless socks, often socks designed specifically for skiing. I've tested two brands: Thor Lo and Fox River. Both make socks that warm, wick, won't wrinkle, and are also padded in the right places for cross-country skiing. (Their snowboard and alpine socks are padded differently.) If your toes are still cold, Grabber and Thermopod sell flameless body-part warmers that give off hours of heat when you most need it. I rarely use them, but I rarely leave home without a couple stuffed in the bottom of my fanny pack, ready for instant first aid.

As for fingers, under all but the most extreme conditions, cross-country skiing generates enough heat to warm them without mittens. About 90 percent of the time, I wear light gloves on my hands and carry heavy gloves or mittens in my pack. And those portable body-part heaters in my fanny pack work for cold hands as well as cold feet.

What else do you need to stay warm? A warm hat is essential equipment, and it becomes more essential as the temperature drops. Your hat stands between you and a 30 to 50 percent heat loss through your head. To protect against frostbite, it must be big enough to pull over your ears—your whole ears right down past the earlobes. When it's too warm for a hat, try an ear jock (technically, ear band), preferably one made of itchless fiber like Turtle Fur. Another heat-loss area is your neck. An itchless neck gaiter will vastly increase your comfort there.

Winter's Diary: November 5

Wash the Windows and It Rains. Before bed I read *Bicycling* magazine from cover to cover, a sure sign it will snow tomorrow.

POSTSKI FOOTWEAR

Good après ski boots are the best way to keep your feet warm before and after skiing. I've tried four types: Polar Treds, Heatraps, Trukks, and mukluks made by Vermont Voyageur in Montgomery Center, Vermont (802-326-4789).

Polar Treds fold up for easy packing and are great to wear in and around the ski lodge. Heatraps aren't quite so portable but have enough tread and support to go tromping around outside. They're really running shoes for winter. Trukks are serious boots—a little hard to get in and out of, but great in deep snow. And the mukluks, which can be worn over street shoes, are high and warm enough for wallowing around in snowdrifts. If you're a winter photographer, they're just the ticket.

SUNGLASSES AND GOGGLES

Look for three things in sunglasses for skiing:

- *UVA and UVB protection.* (Almost all models come with it.)
- *Strength.* Not only do glasses have to resist tree branches and the occasional fall, but skiers are famous for sitting on their glasses in camp and in the car.
- *Dark tint.* Sun and snow make a potently bright combination. Polarized lenses are also useful for blocking sunlight bouncing off the snow.

What you don't want in sunglasses for skiing is a lens that's dark at the top and light at the bottom. They may be fine for driving, but because snow is such an excellent reflector of sunlight, you need all-around protection.

There is no—repeat, no—need to pay $50, $100, or $250 for skiing sunglasses. Cheap, reasonably sturdy ones with UV protection will do just fine. Sooner or later you're gonna end up sitting on them anyway.

But there are times when ordinary sunglasses will not do. In brilliant sunshine, where every surface reflects light, you need wraparounds. They hug the contours of your face and keep reflected light from damaging your eyes. There are a lot of brands out there; get the one that fits best and looks coolest, dude. If you wear prescription glasses, the Bollé Edge is the best model I've found. It comes with snap-out prescription lenses that can be changed as your prescription changes.

Two conditions demand more protection than wraparounds offer. When heavy snow is falling or when it's so cold your bones hurt, you need goggles. Ski goggles help keep your face warm, and they're the best (though still imperfect) way to see through a blizzard. Again, you needn't spring for a top-of-the-line model; if they fit and don't fog up every time you breathe, they'll be fine. If you wear glasses, the Carrera Vision, which fits easily over spectacles, is the best I've found.

5

Striding

Should you find yourself in Oslo, Norway, take a long, steep tram ride from the center of the city to the tram's final stop and Oslo's most prominent landmark, the Holmenkollen Ski Jump. Reaching 100 meters above the mountainside, the jump looks like a giant's beckoning finger, luring adventure seekers to highly adrenalized danger.

At the foot of the jump is the Holmenkollen Ski Museum. Within five minutes of entering its doors, you'll learn a volume about skiing's roots. The museum walls are hung with history: 9-foot-long skis from the early 1800s, birch skis as delicately decorated as scrimshaw, and massive wooden ski poles with a basket at one end and a spear at the other. The basket was used for braking, the spear for hunting bear.

There's also a four-thousand-year-old rock carving from northern Norway, a crude depiction of a man on skis nearly twice as long as he is tall. That carving became the logo of the 1994 Winter

Fig. 18 *Ski museum exhibit*

Olympics at Lillehammer and, as far as we now know, documents the earliest rootlet of classic cross-country skiing.

Quick review: Classic skiing means pushing, or kicking, down and back with one ski in order to drive the other ski forward. At its heart is the diagonal stride, so named because when you kick with your left foot, you pole with your right arm, forming a diagonal line of working muscles (Fig. 19).

Today, classic cross-country skiing is still the method of choice for many skiers under all conditions and for all skiers under many conditions. It's virtually the only way to get through the woods, to handle deep snow, mushy snow, break-through crusted snow. It's the root, the elemental, the source. In a minute I'll show you how to do it. But first a word about what I won't show you.

The difference between this book and many others is that this one doesn't spend a lot of time on detailed instruction. Partly it's because I don't believe most folks get much out of detailed text like "Counter-rotate the upper torso, making sure the shoulders remain perpendicular to the ski, and maintaining the arms and poles parallel to the gliding ski at the point of pole plant." And partly it's because of something that happened last winter.

Fig. 19 *Striding skier*

We had December visitors, John and Colleen from New Zealand. Neither had ever been on skis; both were well past forty. On their first day I put them on nordic skis in the backyard, gave them the same sort of basic instruction I'm about to give you, and set them loose.

They loved it. They wallowed in it! The next day we drove to a cross-country ski center to give them the experience of track skiing. I continued my minimalist instruction, offering them a single pointer every time I passed them on the big oval track. They were doing great, learning fast, and having a blast.

But we weren't alone on the track. A real instructor with perfect technique, Lycra clothes, and zero body fat was instructing a couple of guys in their early twenties. With every stride, he corrected their technique. He told them everything they were doing wrong. He showed them precisely how it should be done. He made them repeat it until they got it right.

Within ten minutes, the two guys could barely move without falling. They were clearly having no fun. And they were paying to learn that they were klutzes who would obviously never be in the same league as the instructor.

They were victims of overinstruction. And though I freely acknowledge that racers might require the kind of detailed training that will give them a few seconds' advantage, I contend that nonracers do better with minimal instruction. Cross-country skiing is a simple sport, not astrophysics. It's easy, fun, and quick to learn. Don't let purists deprive you of that.

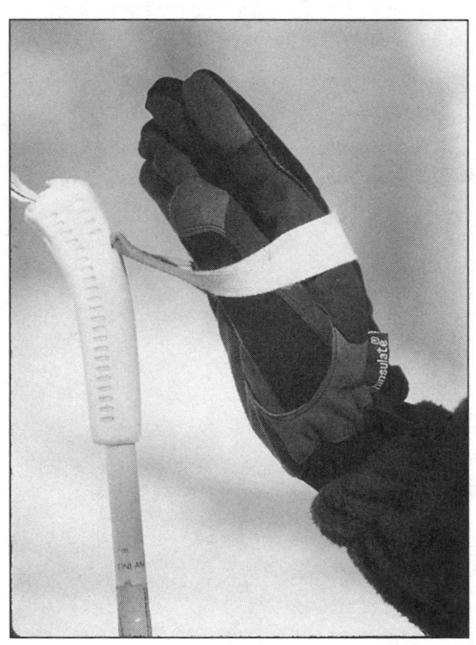

Fig. 20 *Hand on pole*

End of sermon. Let's go skiing.

First, get into your skis and poles. If you've bought step-in bindings (which you should have unless you're telemarking or doing heavy-duty backcountry bushwhacking), here's how. On level ground, and using your poles for balance, line up the steel bar on the front of one boot with the crevice in the ski binding. Step down until you hear a satisfying snap. Now the other binding. *Snap.* Now slip your hands up through the adjustable straps on the handle of your poles.

A QUICK NOTE ABOUT OUR MODEL

Were we lucky! Instead of using a brother-in-law or the kid down the road to model techniques, we got Pepa Miloucheva, the former world ski orienteering champion. Pepa learned skiing on the Bulgarian National Ski Team and moved to our backyard at the end of 1996. Our "backyard" is the Craftsbury Outdoor Center, where Pepa's a much-in-demand instructor and masseuse, and where the photos of her were taken. If you are the kind of learner who studies pictures in detail, you can be certain that the photos in this chapter show technique at its very best.

Adjust the strap so that you're comfortable, the strap isn't cutting off your circulation, and you have enough slack in the strap to let go of the pole completely when you swing your hand back, but not so much that the handle slips out of your hands when you open your fingers.

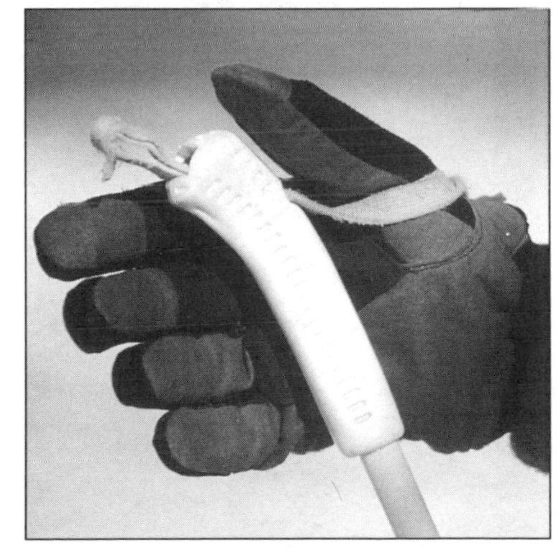

Fig. 22 *Pole grip*

Stand comfortably on your skis, knees slightly bent, hands by your sides, poles pointing behind you. You're in the basic athletic position (Fig. 23).

Fig. 23 *Basic athletic position*

Fig. 24 *Basic skier's position*

Now bend your knees a little more, bring your hands a few inches forward, and lean slightly forward from ankles, knees, and waist. That's the basic skier's position (Fig. 24).

You're still on level ground, not a steep hillside, and you're not too hot and not freezing to death. Smile—you're gonna have fun. You're about to take your first classic stride.

Reach forward with your right arm. Plant your right pole a few inches outside the ball of your right ski boot. Push down and back with your right foot. Glide forward on your left ski (Fig. 25).

Hey, that's it—you're skiing! Now try the same sequence on the other side. Plant left pole. Push off with left foot. Glide on right ski. Bravo! Before long, you'll stop thinking of each plant-push-glide as a separate movement and realize that it's one step in a dance. When the glide begins to slow (and friction plus the laws of physics pretty much guarantee that it will slow), plant-push-glide on the other side. You're getting into the flow, the rhythm that is cross-country skiing.

This is a sport you can learn to do in a morning—in an hour if you have a reasonable sense of balance. It's also a sport you can spend your life perfecting, always stealing a bit more glide, always improving the thrust of the pole, the kick of the driving foot.

Fig. 25 *First stride*

What's the best way to improve? There are two. One is to stay on one ski for longer and longer glides. The other is to practice skiing without poles. Gliding on one ski does wonders for your sense of balance. At first it feels awkward, like you're gonna fall every time you raise the other ski off the snow. Sometimes you might. That's OK. Snow is (usually) soft, speeds are (usually) slow, and falling is as much a part of skiing as striking out is part of baseball.

How do you learn to balance on one ski? Think TKN: toe, knee, nose. Instead of centering your

Fig. 26 *TKN (back view)*

Fig. 27 *TKN close-up*

body between your skis, lean it out over the gliding ski so that if you dropped a plumb line from your nose, your knee would cross it and then your toes (Fig. 26). Unless you're a dancer, TKN is not going to feel like a natural stance, so practice until it does.

Nothing is better for improving your stride than poleless skiing (Fig. 28). Most skiers rely too heavily on their poles for balance and drive. Better to use those big thigh muscles than your relatively puny arms for propulsion. It's more efficient and considerably less tiring. This applies to striding and skating alike.

There are ski experts who will tell you precisely how much energy should be coming from your legs (80 percent is one figure) and how much from your arms. I don't believe in such precision. For one thing, I have no idea how you'd measure such a ratio; for another, unless you're a serious racer, it's fine to find a ratio that suits your style. As a rule, work toward getting more power from your skis and less from your poles.

The two biggest impediments to better skiing are downcast eyes and hidden hands. It's natural to want to look down at what those strange, long things on your feet are up to, but once you've satisfied your curiosity, look up. Keep your eyes focused on the trail ahead—not just to see where you're going (though that's nice, too), but also to keep your posture upright and balanced.

Fig. 28 *Striding without poles*

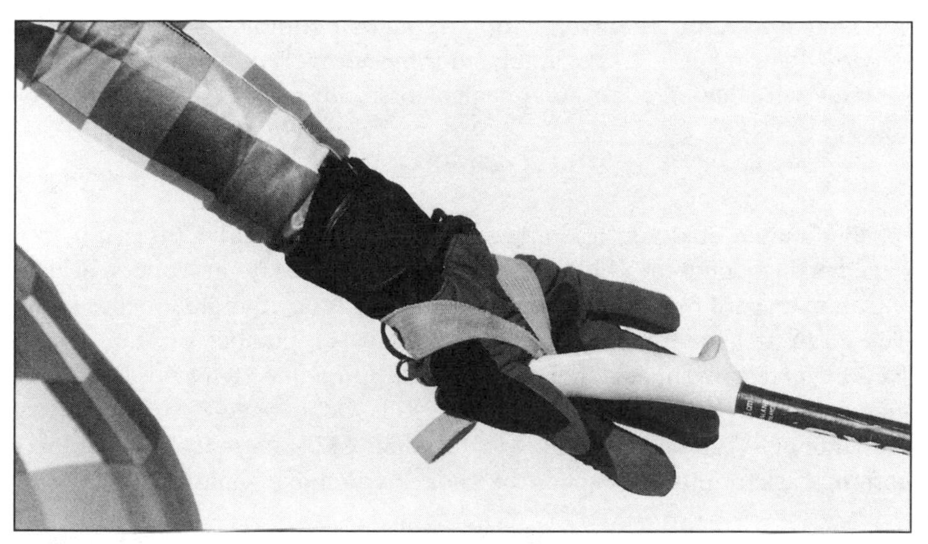

Fig. 29 *Loose hand grip*

When you're going downhill, your hands, should be in front of you, leading your body into a turn. They almost automatically keep the rest of you in proper balance. That's why it's so important to keep them where you can see them. If your hands fall behind you, it's only a matter of time before you fall, too.

Tension is a thief of energy. The looser you can be, the more energy you'll have for skiing. One way tension expresses itself is in the pole grip. If you find yourself holding onto your pole as if it's the only thing between you and sudden death (and if you're a new skier, the odds are that's exactly what you're doing), relax that grip of iron. Hold the poles lightly when you're planting them, and not at all when you're not. How do you do that? By letting the strap do the holding. When you swing your arm forward before a pole plant and back after a pole plant, the wrist strap will hold the pole for you. That's precisely what it's there for (Fig. 29).

Some things seem too obvious to mention. They're often the ones that need mentioning most. So here are two obvious things that will speed you on your way to skiing pleasure.

- Tighten your laces. Start them tight, and as the day goes on, tighten them again. It's the easiest way to improve your edge control and reduce unexpected falls. As a bonus, snug-fitting boots greatly reduce the likelihood of developing blisters.
- Keep breathing. Nothing tightens you up more than holding your breath, say at the top of a steep hill. Nothing loosens you faster than breathing in, breathing out; breathing in, breathing out . . . Singing helps, too.

Here is a mantra that works for striding and gliding, for beginners and experts. Remember it. These are the four most important words in the book —that's why they're about to appear before your eyes in big, bold letters. Ready?

GO FOR THE GLIDE.

No matter what you're doing—striding across a field, skiing in tracks, even herringboning up a hill—try to extend your glide time. Work on achieving an extra yard or at least an extra inch every time your ski touches snow. The glide is at the heart of skiing; it's what distinguishes this sport from walking and snowshoeing. ("In snowshoeing, you need ten steps to become an expert and eleven to get bored," says Bill Dodge, cross-country product manager at Salomon.) The glide is the bonus of pleasure that keeps skiers coming back for more. So go for the glide. It will make you grin.

Fig. 30 *Gliding*

FALLING

Falling will also make you grin. Oh yes, you will fall. You *should* fall. Falling is a fact of skiing. It is not a problem. In fact, it's all to the good. On alpine or cross-country skis, I don't really relax until after my first fall of the season.

Remember my New Zealand friends, John and Colleen, the couple I taught to ski? Here's something I didn't tell you. As they circled the track on

Fig. 31 *Fallen skier*

their second day on skis, I came upon them and asked, "How you doing?"

"Box of birds," said John. "Box of fluffy ducks." (New Zealandese for "Fine, just fine.")

"Good," I said. "Now relax." And with that I pushed him into the soft snow.

John looked surprised but unhurt. "Nice," I said. "You fell nice and relaxed, just as you should. Now I'll show you how to get up."

Like John, unless you're falling on ice or inch-thick crust, you're in for a pleasant surprise—because snow is soft and forgiving, falling usually doesn't hurt. The trick is getting back up.

If you've fallen to the side on relatively level ground, it's not much of a trick. Put your skis beneath your butt, push down on the snow with your gloved hand, and up you go.

Fig. 32 *Rising skier*

Fig. 33a

Fig. 33b

Fig. 33c

Fig. 33d

But suppose you've taken a megafall, say a face plant on a steep slope. Here's the trick. First, disentangle your skis and poles. Once you've found where your body parts lie, roll on your back or side until your skis are below your body and facing across the hill. Then push yourself up with your uphill arm—the one closest to the top of the slope. Stand up, dust off, blow nose, wipe goggles, and—ta da!—resume skiing.

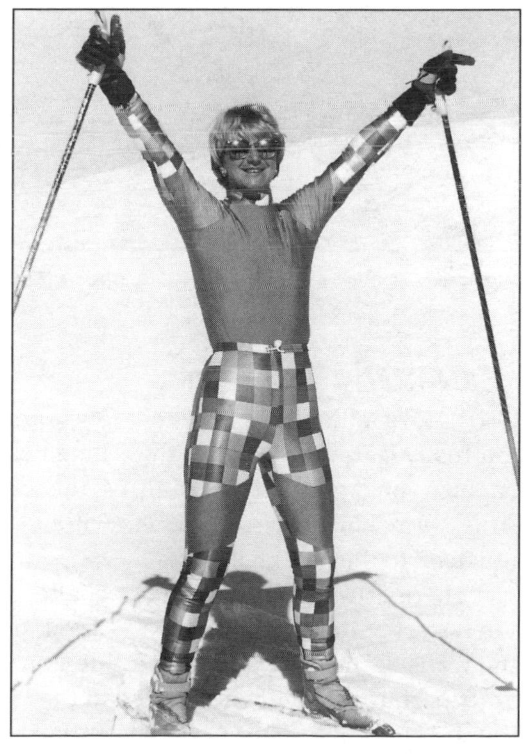

Fig. 33e

Fig. 33a–e
Getting up from stomach

In the rare event that the snow is so deep that your pushing hand sinks in up to the shoulder, unhitch your poles, cross them, and use them as a platform from which to push yourself up (Fig. 34). (But not if you've bought those lightweight, expensive graphite poles. Lean on them and they'll break in two.)

Fig. 34 *Crossed poles*

TURNING ON THE LEVEL

OK, you've fallen, gotten up, and now you're skiing straight and on the level, gradually learning the feel of these long boards on your feet, improving your balance, and getting the hang of the power kick. Once you're linking strides—making forward progress without a stop between kicks—it's time to move on to the next challenge.

There actually are three next challenges: uphill, downhill, and turns. We'll start with turns on relatively level ground. If you're skiing in a track, the walls of the track will help guide your ski around the turn. You can do your part by turning your ankles so that your toes—and ski tips—point in the direction of the curve. Turn your face and shoulders in the same direction. Sounds easy, doesn't it? It is. The only trick is trusting that the process will work. It will, though it may take you three or four times of watching it work to believe it.

When you're not in a track, you have several level turning options. The first, and often the best, is simplicity itself. Lift your ski off the snow and aim it in the direction you wish to turn. To avoid crossing your skis, lift the right ski for right turns, the left for left turns.

Start by doing this simple maneuver when you're not moving. Plant your poles beside you, lift the right ski, and angle it in the direction you want to turn (Fig. 36). Then return it to the snow, put your weight on it, and ski off in the new direction.

Congratulations. You've just completed a step turn. Once that feels comfortable—and it won't take long—do the same maneuver while you're moving. That's a

Fig. 35 *Skier in turning track*

Fig. 36 *Step turn*

gliding step turn, or skating turn. Here's how it works. You're gliding on the left ski, and remembering TKN, so all your weight is on it. While you're gliding, lift the tip of the right ski and set it down in the direction you want to turn. Now, shift all your weight onto your right ski. As your glide slows, drive off the right ski and proceed in your new direction. That sudden smile that wreaths your face is the sign that you've got it.

But to really impress your friends, you need to learn the kick turn. Let's say you've gotten a *leetle* out of control and have come to a stop facing directly into the unwelcoming branches of a pine tree. Don't worry—one quick kick turn, and your back will be to the branches. The kick turn reverses direction with an elegant, show-offy maneuver (Fig. 37a– d). Here's how to do it:

Plant your left pole beside the tip of your left ski, right pole between the tails of both skis. (I know other books say outside the right ski; my way works better.) Lift high the tip of your right ski, swivel it 180 degrees, and lay it on the snow. Your skis are still parallel, only presently they're tip to tail. Now, in one fluid motion, swing the left ski around. You are now facing in the exact opposite direction you were but a short moment before.

The kick turn is more than a party trick. Whether you are

37a-d Kick turn

Fig. 37a

Fig. 37b

Fig. 37c

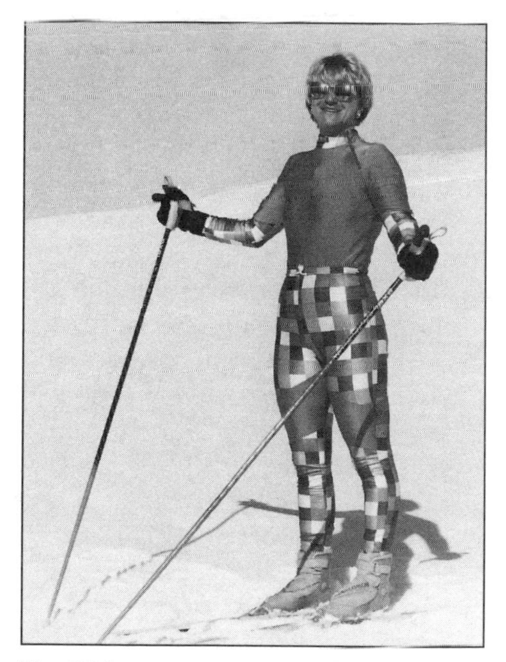

Fig. 37d

ascending or descending a steep, wide slope, it's the most efficient way to change direction. On a line no steeper than you're comfortable with, traverse across the slope. Stop. Kick turn. Now traverse back to the other side. Voilà—fearless skiing!

SKIING UPHILL

Now it's time to tackle the nordic miracle—skiing uphill. Because of the kick wax or the scales under your feet, when you come to a hill, you are able to continue the same sort of striding you've been doing on the level. If you've got just the right wax on or an aggressive scale pattern, you can stride up remarkably steep hills without slipping backward. There's that smile again!

But at some point, your skis may become prisoners of gravity. For every step you take forward and upward, they'll slide an equal or greater distance back down. Unless you know what to do, it can be downright discouraging.

Here's what to do: Start by splaying the tips of your skis outward so that your track up the hill makes a herringbone pattern. This is called, for obvious reasons, *herringboning* (Fig. 38). It takes over when gravity proves too much for grip. At first, make narrow Vs up the hill. Then, as the slope grows steeper, spread them wider. With each step, set the inner edge of the ski into the

Fig. 38 *Herringbone*

Fig. 39 *Sidestepping*

snow so that instead of fighting gravity, you're
creating a double stairway to the stars.

When gravity eventually overcomes herringboning, the next movement is *sidestepping* (Fig. 39). Bracing yourself with the downhill pole and hauling yourself with the uphill, you progress step by step up the hill. Instead of facing forward, you're facing sideways. It sounds awkward. It *is* awkward. Particularly in heavy snow, sidestepping is heavy going. It's hard work and painfully slow, which is why it's the movement of last resort. Sidestepping is both slower and much less efficient than herringboning, and herringboning is slower and less efficient than normal striding. So use them only when you need to.

Ah, but how do you know when you need to? A lot of skiers never find out. As soon as they see a rise, they break out of their stride and into a herringbone or sidestep. Don't do this. Stay in stride as long as you're able. Look for gentler paths to the top. Put extra power in your kick. Use your poles to keep you from sliding backward. Try running on skis. Only when all that fails should you switch to the less efficient methods of propulsion.

As when herringboning, don't lay your skis flat on the slope when sidestepping up a hill.

Instead, drive them edge-first into the snow. It's easier to climb a stairway than to scale a slippery slope.

When moving to the next stair, especially if the snow is heavy and deep, here's another tip: Don't raise your ski straight up. Instead, angle your ankle and slide it out. That way, instead of lifting 2 feet of snow every time you take a step, all you lift is your ski. The angled ski dumps the snow before emerging into the air.

Fig. 40 *Angled ski emerging from snow*

SKIING DOWNHILL

Now it's time to try what for many is the scariest part of cross-country skiing: going down hills. Even if you already know how to downhill on alpine skis, get ready for a new learning experience. With their steel edges and locked heels, alpine skis make downhill sliding relatively easy. Going too fast? Dig in those edges, angle your ankles, and turn. Turning is the best way out of what every sane skier fears—too much speed.

But most cross-country skis have no metal edges. And though free heels are great for climbing hills, they lack a lot when you are trying to turn your way out of excessive speed on the way down. So what do you do?

The first and best defense is to increase your tolerance for speed. Turn what was terrifying into something exhilarating. Learn to enjoy speeding straight down a hill.

Note that "hill" is different from "cliff" and that if there's a creek or a tree or an angry bull at the bottom of said hill, this might not be the moment for speed. But most of the time, there's no bull, no tree, and the hills are not as steep as they appear. As I discovered in Quebec.

I first learned to alpine ski in the Laurentian Mountains of Quebec. My third day on skis, I rode the high-speed T-bar at Mont Gabriel. With fear and trembling, I observed that the ride up was so steep that my ski tips were level with my eyes. Two years later, I returned to the mountain and discovered that on the same T-bar, my tips were now level with my knees. Either I had grown 5 feet or my perception had changed with experience.

Yours will, too. Choose a hill with a longish run-out at the bottom, and spend a morning acclimating to steepness. Start at your own point of comfort, maybe 50 feet up, and ski straight down. On the next run, start a few feet higher. Work your way up until you enjoy what seemed so terrifying just a short time before. This is one of the best things you can do to increase your enjoyment of skiing.

David Goodman is an award-winning ski writer who does everything on nordic skis. Through the woods, over the mountain, across the frozen lake, Goodman and his free heels have been there, done that, got the mukluk. Here's Goodman on going down:

"Speed is fun. Wind rushing through your hair is a good thing. But beyond that, the ability to go down opens up whole swatches of previously forbidden terrain. When I started cross-country skiing, the word *downhill* evoked one emotion only—terror. The simple reality was, to go downhill was to give up whatever semblance of control I had on these frail things called skis.

"Then I discovered something: There was more to life than floppy boots and skinny skis. With the benefit of a sturdy boot and a metal-edged ski, I could actually stay in the vertical world. Now, going downhill had another meaning—joy.

"Throw in a telemark or a parallel turn, and you have all the ingredients for poetry in motion. Learning to downhill liberates us from the confines of gentle valley floors and logging roads. By adding a third dimension to our skiing, we can now travel anywhere that is white."

SLOWING DOWN

But you'd also better learn how to slow down when you need to. There are a number of ways to do this.

First, you can fall. Unless you're on a slope way too steep for normal cross-country skiing, this will break your speed without breaking your body. Admittedly, falling lacks a certain elegance, but I'm not ashamed to say I've used it as an emergency bailout on many occasions.

How do you fall? Make a quick check to ensure that no rock protrudes from the snow at the point you plan to make contact, and get your butt down. Your butt, not your hand. Butt injuries are a lot less common than wrist injuries, and you'll finally find out why you're so well padded there. Relax, and try to fall to the side so you don't land on your skis. Remember, the object is to cut speed, not add to it.

Fig. 41 *Snowplow*

Slightly up the elegance scale from falling is snowplowing, a.k.a. wedging. Essentially, this is slowing down by scraping the snow with your skis. It ain't pretty, and the next day you'll find inner thigh muscles you never knew you owned, but snowplowing works. It puts on the brakes. And it's not hard to learn.

Start on a gentle hill. Form a pizza wedge with your skis: tips nearly touching, tails splayed out, knees bent and a foot apart. Bend your knees so that your inside edges are in contact with the snow (Fig. 41). Start sliding down the hill. Notice how slow you're going. That's what you want.

Straighten your skis, get out of the snowplow, and keep heading downhill, and you quickly pick up speed. Now sink back into the snowplow. You slow down again. Straight skis—fast. Pizza skis—slow. Practice until you can snowplow on steeper terrain and without your thighs begging for mercy.

But what if you're not just skiing down a hill, but skiing down a hill with set tracks? You can't snowplow in tracks!

True. But there's something you can do. You can lift one ski out of the track and execute a one-footed snowplow (Fig. 42). You don't get quite the braking power, but it will still keep you from achieving terminal velocity without the indignity of dragging your butt through the tracks. Give one-footed plowing a try.

One last scenario: Let's say you're skiing too fast down a too-steep slope. You're moving too swiftly for effective snowplowing, and daggerlike protruding rocks pretty much eliminate the sitting-down maneuver. What to do?

Fig. 42 *One-foot snowplow*

Pull out a trick from skiing's past: Use your poles as a snow anchor. Grab them together in both hands—one hand on the handles, the other down near the baskets. Now jam the points into the snow beside you, and press like hell until your speed drops.

SPEEDING UP

Now that you know how to slow down, you can work on speeding up. On long, not-too-steep downhills, the most elegant way to achieve this is through the tuck. With knees slightly bent, back parallel to the snow, hands in front, pole tips behind, weight on your whole feet, you'll feel like a racer (Fig. 43). And the next day, you'll discover thigh muscles you never knew you owned. For extra speed, sit back on your heels.

Fig. 43 *Tuck*

Fig. 44a

Fig. 44 b

Fig. 44 a–c *Double pole*

When the trail's not steep enough for a tuck, try double-poling (Fig. 44a–c). Classic striding doesn't work well on downhills, so the best strategy is to switch from leg power to upper-body power. Assume the position: feet together, arms straight out in front, poles planted by your feet. Keeping your arms nearly straight, which is important to maximize their power, push down and back. Following through, bend forward at the waist and let your poles sail out behind you.

Fig. 44c

Then start again. Keep going without stopping. As you pole, think about building a rhythm. As long as you're skiing downhill, you can move surprisingly fast without any help from your legs.

When the trail approaches flat, you can try a variation, the double-pole single step (Fig. 45). This time, kick as you pole (which is why it's also known as a double pole with kick).

Fig. 45 *Double-pole, single step*

Play with these and other variations. Remember, the object is to propel yourself with reasonable efficiency and grace, not to execute a perfect double-pole single step or any other textbook movement.

DOWNHILL TURNS

Going downhill, you can use the same turns as on the level, but because gravity is helping you along, you can add other turns to your repertoire. The most specialized turn is the telemark turn. It's so specialized, a whole chapter is devoted to it. Save it for later.

The most basic turn is the *wedge turn* (sometimes called the snowplow turn). Once you've learned how to snowplow, it's easy. Get into your pizza position. Start down the hill. Then put all your weight on your left foot—

all of it! Count slowly to five, and by the time you reach three, you'll notice something remarkable is happening. Your left ski is turning right. Keep weighting it. Even more remarkable, it's turning so far it's eventually headed uphill. Keep weighting it. And now, miracle of miracles, you come to a complete stop. Congratulations—you've just completed your first wedge turn (Fig. 46, 47).

Fig. 46 *Left wedge*

Do the same thing with the right ski, then the left, then the right, then the left, until the wedge turn becomes an arrow you can pull from your quiver any time you need it.

I'll acknowledge that though a wedge turn moves you in the direction you wish to go and slows you down at the same time, it is not a lissome maneuver. No one ever felt sexy while locked in a wedge, nor has anyone felt graceful. To experience these feelings, you need to move up to the stem turn and, prettier still, the parallel turn. I'm about to give you the drill on both, but before I do, consider an unorthodox way of looking at the whole turning issue.

Fig. 47 *Right wedge*

Instead of thinking, first I learn to wedge, then to stem, then to parallel, picture these three turns not as separate, discrete maneuvers but as points on a continuum. You start with the wedge because it's usually considered the easiest to learn. But rather than practicing it to perfection before moving on to the other turns, get a rough hang of the way it feels, then start fiddling with it. The tune you're fiddling should go like this:

I'm a-aimin' to git my skis,
Runnin' straight beneath my knees.
With jes' the littlest correction,
They'll go in the same di-recshun.
I'm a-gonna laugh at dirty weather,
When my skis are turnin' together.*

What the song means is that the object is to keep your skis parallel to one another as often as you can, for as long as you can. When you can make a turn by wedging only one ski, you're stemming. When you can comfortably turn both skis in the same direction at roughly the same time, you're paralleling. Start playing with this idea just as soon as you can quickly and comfortably sink into a wedge turn.

Here's how to do it, beginning with the stem turn. The difference between the stem and the wedge is this: When you're wedging, your skis are

Fig. 48a

Fig. 48b

*Author's note: This is an actual country/western tune.

always angled like a slice of pizza; when you're stemming, your skis are parallel for the time between turns.

In the first *stem turn* (sometimes called the christie or the basic turn), your skis are parallel to one another as you traverse to the right. Then you plant your left pole and step your right leg out to form the pizza slice. You weight that ski, and a moment later you change directions and once again have your skis running parallel (Fig. 48a–c).

The next turn to learn is the *parallel turn*. Here pizza wedge has disappeared completely. Now the skis turn together. To make that happen, you need to point your knees in the direction of the turn and steer your feet around the curve (Fig. 49a–b).

Make the parallel movement more extreme and you'll execute a *hockey stop* (Fig. 50), complete with showers of snow and awed spectators. Alpine skiers should note that this is a lot harder trick to perform on edgeless skinny skis; it might be wise to practice in private before attempting to wow your friends.

Fig. 48a–c *Stem turn*

Fig. 48c

Fig. 49a

Fig. 49b

Fig. 49a–b *Parallel turn*

Fig. 50 *Hockey stop*

6

Skating

Skating has become a major factor in cross-country skiing only in the last two decades of the twentieth century. The technique itself isn't new; it's always been an efficient means of locomotion for short stretches on level ground.

But sometime around 1980, cross-country racers started skating for longer periods on more types of terrain. And skaters began winning races against diagonal striders. Skating got its start in the United States when American ski racer Bill Koch learned it from Swedish competitors and then surprised the world by using it to win the World Cup in 1982.

Fig. 51 *Skating skier*

Soon it became so popular that racing associations had to divide competitions into classic and freestyle. In the former, racers were required to maintain diagonal striding for most of the course; in the latter, anything went—and went fast.

Says John Brodhead, director of skiing at the Craftsbury Out-

Fig. 52 *Champion runner Joan Benoit after her first cross-country ski race*

door Center in Craftsbury, Vermont, and an avid amateur racer: "Cross-country ski racing is about power and finesse. A well-designed course is like a roller-coaster ride where you provide the momentum. The uphills are as satisfying as the downhills. You are in control: rocketing down a narrow, twisty trail at speeds up to 40 miles per hour, cutting to the inside of turns just inches from the edge, maintaining your speed through the transitions, coming out of your tuck at just the right moment to power up and over the next hill, and maintaining your rhythm as you blast past the racer who started thirty seconds ahead of you.

"Every stride is different. Speed is a result of the application of power in just the right amount and direction depending on the ever-changing undulations of the track. Every muscle in your body is working to propel you forward. You balance on just one ski at a time. The ski is 45 millimeters wide, weighs just a few ounces, and glides over a packed track like a hot knife on butter.

"The satisfaction of fast cross-country skis on a well-prepared track is immense. If you are fit, have good technique, and good equipment, cross-country ski racing is never boring. Bill Koch, the only U.S. cross-country ski Olympic medalist, in a moment of unbridled enthusiasm about the sport, once said, 'If everybody could cross-country ski, the world would be a better place.' "

As skating took hold, form swiftly followed function, and a new kind of ski evolved. Gone was the kick zone, the wax pocket, the ski designed to stop, grip, and go. In its place emerged a ski designed with only one function—to go and keep on going. The change came because skaters continued to outrace diagonal striders. It spread to recreational skiers, who discovered that they could skate along snowmobile trails, on firm snow away from set tracks, and in marginal conditions when the snow was too soft or too wet for striding. They also found that skating takes more effort and makes for bigger thigh muscles that ripple appealingly under Lycra.

Quick review: Skating on skis is very much like skating on ice skates. In both sports, you start your glide by pointing blade or ski outward and pushing off a moving foot. In classic skiing, your skis move straight ahead. In skating, they are always moving away from each other. Because only one ski at a time touches the snow, you progress between them.

How do you skate? Remember the step turn you learned for classic skiing? The one where you set off in a new direction by pointing the ski, then gliding off on it? Good news—you're halfway to learning to skate.

Fig. 53a

Fig. 53a–c *Skating*

Fig. 53b

Fig. 53c

The other half is to repeat the motion in the other direction. In skating, you don't move in the direction you want to go; you angle off on either side of it. Skating is more like ice skating than classic striding. The trouble is, instead of having shoe-length skates on your feet, you have many-times-shoe-length skis. That makes for initial awkwardness and almost guarantees you'll cross tips and tails more than once as you learn to cope with this gigantic footwear. One way of making the process quicker and easier is to learn on short skating skis.

So one way skating differs from striding is that your skis are always moving on an angle. Another difference is in how you use your poles. Striders use them one at a time: left pole, right ski; right pole, left ski. Skaters usually use both poles together. On every other glide, or sometimes every glide, you plant both pole tips in the snow and push off. Sounds like a pretty good upper-body workout? The next morning you'll find out just how good it was.

About this "every other glide or sometimes every glide" thing: They're called V1 and V2. All it means is that sometimes you pole on every push-off, sometimes on every other push-off. Poling every time gives more speed and more climbing power but at the cost of greater expenditure of energy. How do you know when to V1 and when to V2? By experience. Play with both. Play with going four push-offs between pole plants. As long as you're willing to experiment and play, you learn to ski by skiing.

Classic skiers stride in the tracks, whereas skating skiers skate in the groomed path beside the tracks. But sometimes you'll see someone coming along with one ski in the track and one ski in the path. What gives?

Fig. 54 *Marathon*

What you're seeing is the marathon skate, an energy-saving technique for long-distance skiing (Fig. 54). Marathoning isn't hard to do, merely hard to get used to. Here, the in-track ski is doing the gliding and the out-of-track ski is doing the pushing.

The reason this book's skating section is so much shorter than the striding section is that many of the basics are the same for both. Take TKN, for example: Toe, knee,

Fig. 55a Fig. 55a–b *TKN* Fig. 55b

and nose need to be lined up in skating as well. Your whole body should follow your ski (55a–b).

One of the most common skating mistakes is to let your body hover between skis. As in striding, efficient skating demands a commitment to get your body over the gliding ski. One way to achieve it is to look in the direction your ski is pointing.

Another common mistake is to raise the skis too high off the snow. Don't do that; it takes too much energy. Just lift them an inch or so. That's enough. You'll be better balanced and not so tired at the end of the day.

Fig. 56 *Skate efficiency*

Efficiency also demands that as you switch from ski to ski, you set the new gliding ski down in front of the old one. If you've never skated this way, you'll feel an immediate increase in power. If you've never been able to skate uphill, you may be in for a pleasant surprise.

People often want to know whether they can skate on striding skis and stride on skating skis. Purists say no. I say yes. You'll lose efficiency both ways, but have no doubt, it can be done. It's fun to do, and I do it all the time. Remember, cross-country skiing is a low-tech, low-impact sport. You can have fun on a pair of old hickory boards you find in the attic. Don't let the pursuit of purism rob you of your pleasure.

Winter's Diary: November 6

Snow Walk. Remember I said reading a bike magazine would bring snow? Worked again! I wake up to 2 inches of swirling white. This time I don't offer any resistance. While Effin writes the Great American Children's Story, Marsha and I lace up our boots. The thermometer says 18, so we scrape away the klister, twigs, and dirt and apply a new layer of green wax.

On my fiberglass Rossignols, the wax works moderately well. As long as I keep moving, I can glide. But on Marsha's old Norwegian hickory skis, the wax does no good at all. In fact, she isn't skiing, she's walking on snow. And carrying snow. By the time we quit, she has clumps so thick that the encased skis look like pigs in a blanket.

Do we care? Hell, no—we're skiing in early November!

7

The Backcountry

If I had to choose between on- and off-trail skiing, I would, after protesting that I had to make the choice, swiftly opt for off trail. Off-trail, or backcountry, skiing is done in parks, backyards, farmers' fields, and the great outdoors, rather than at ski areas. I'm lucky enough to live where I can ski from the back door, and I do it, at least for an hour or so, most days of winter. While few Americans enjoy this luxury (or the 100 inches of snow I push off my driveway each winter), there are at least a couple of days each year when many Americans—and many days when most Canadians—can ski without driving first.

Fig. 57 *Crested Butte, Colorado*

Not driving to ski is one of the great advantages cross-country skiers enjoy over alpine adventurers. And it's an advantage off-trail skiers enjoy over set-track skiers. Another pleasure open to off-trailers is solitude. For me, that's a shared solitude—me, my wife, our dog, and sometimes a couple of friends or daughters thrown in for added pleasure. A third delight is the feeling that as you turn your skis down a long hill on which cows were munching clover three months ago, you may well be the first person, ever, to ski that line. Ever.

If you like challenge, try bushwhacking. I did some early-spring bushwhacking along the northernmost stretch of Vermont's Catamount Trail, which will eventually traverse the state from the Massachusetts line all the way to Canada. But when I joined a party of backcountry skiers on that last leg, long sections of the Catamount existed only in the minds of the planners. Here's what it was like . . .

By early afternoon the thermometer had climbed to 50, and the snow was thick as honey. We slogged through drifts, waded through puddles, and

Fig. 58 *Sophie*

removed our skis when the snow ran out, which it did about fourteen times. We also had to cross a substantial stream, swift and swollen with spring runoff. Just when I was about to regretfully observe that we would have to turn back, Rolf found the last unmelted snow bridge. One by one, we gingerly skied across. I waited until all the others had made it safely across before taking my turn. After all, I was the one with the camera.

We headed into the last American woods at 1:30. We emerged from the last American woods at 4:30. In between, we got lost, retraced our tracks, got lost again, then hacked our way through miles of the thorniest puckerbrush in the state of Vermont. I've encountered killer cactus with duller needles.

Finally, we emerged at the top of a hill overlooking the border town of North Troy. Taking a collective deep breath, we aimed our skis down the hill and north of the town, to what Rolf assured us was the Canadian border. By now the slushy snow had firmed up considerably, and our speed of descent was downright impressive.

But however impressive I felt, when my skis got ahead of me 50 feet from the bottom, I rapidly lost my footing, my nerve, and any trace of impressiveness, in that order. I hit a 3-inch-deep puddle with a splash, then hit the frozen ground beneath it with a thud. I was soaked from my gurgle to my zatch.

That's bushwhacking—wet snow, frozen snow, no snow; lost trails, lost footing, lost nerve; wet bottoms, bruised bottoms . . . and great, great memories.

It should be obvious from my description of the day that backcountry skiing means taking the snow as it comes. To some extent, that's true of ski-area skiing as well—you can encounter ice and slush at cross-country centers and alpine resorts alike. But ski areas have machines to maximize snow conditions; in the outback, there's only nature.

Now, some of that natural snow is the sweetest stuff you'll ever experience. It can give you the sensation of skiing through bolts of silk, bales of cotton, slinky sheets of satin. Or, it can give you the sensation of skiing over blocks of ice, mounds of crud, rinds of breakable crust. Let's look at how to handle these, uh, challenging conditions. Starting with ice.

ICE

My first-line advice is simplicity itself: Read a book. No, not about how to ski ice—*instead* of skiing ice. Stay home by the fire with hot cocoa and a good book. Ice is hard enough to handle on alpine skis with scalpel edges and clamped-down heels; on ordinary cross-country skis, it's pure torture.

Still, ice happens. And there are times when it can't be avoided. Here's a strategy for getting by.

You're skiing down a steep trail, and there in front of you is what you'd hoped never to see: A stream crossing the trail has thawed, then refrozen, leaving a band of ice 10 feet wide that must be crossed. You look for your first line of defense—skiing around it—and discover that the band goes on forever. There *is* no around it. You consider taking off your skis, but the stuff looks so slick that it might be harder to negotiate on ski boots than on skis. Other than wait for spring, what do you do?

The answer is, as little as you can. It's an old alpine skier's trick: When you encounter ice, don't turn, don't slow down, don't stop—just ski straight over it, staying as relaxed as you can manage. When it's safely behind you, that's the time to make your directional and speed adjustments. The motto for unavoidable ice: Get over it!

ICING

The phenomenon known as icing is not related to traveling on ice but usually comes in the form of snow that clumps on the bottom of your ski. In certain conditions—usually, warm and wet ones—great mounds of snow cling to the skis, defying gravity and soon defying you to ski on them.

The first line of defense against icing is glide waxing. To prevent icing on top of skis, wax there as well. Avoid icing by sidestepping around puddles and streams. Cure icing (at least temporarily) by scraping the bottom of one ski across the top of the other.

HEAVY, WET SNOW

Traveling over heavy, wet snow, often known as crud, requires skills beyond patience, in part because unlike a narrow icy band, crud often doesn't quit. You can start the day skiing crud and six hours later still be skiing crud.

Also known as white trash, sludge, pudding, and Sierra cement, this thick, heavy, waterlogged snow can suck your ski like a giant octopus. The best equipment for mastering crud is the sturdiest, stiff, shaped skis with telemark bindings and supportive boots. To ski crud, you need to take charge, to boss it around. You need to—and here's the motto for crud—kick butt!

What this means is increasing the power of every move. Your turns must be more forceful. Your up-and-down motion must be exaggerated. When crud is really deep and gluelike, you may have to actually hop the tails of your skis clear of it on every turn. There's another motto—leap and land!

With crud, use your poles to get you up, down, and around; your upper body to initiate the turning movement; your arms to give your turns more force. As crud expert Allan Bard put it, you need "a well-anticipated upper-body position, undaunted faith, and a good primal growl."

CRUST

And growling brings us to the third great challenge of ungroomed snow: crust. Crust comes in two varieties, breakable and unbreakable. The latter usually presents no problems. You ski on top of it, which usually means a speedy ride with lots of glide and not much kick. It's not as slick as ice, but if you fall, it's sure not as soft as powder.

Breakable crust is another story. If it breaks easily, it too presents few problems. The first run is slow and awkward, but once you've reached your destination, you can turn around and ski back in the perfect tracks you've laid. It's sweet skiing through sweetheart snow.

Ah, but when crust breaks hard, that's when the troubles start. Picture it: You're skiing fast and easy on a firm, slick surface. You give a mighty kick, but instead of gliding, your ski dives. And stops. Short. Unless you have reflexes of greased lightning, your body hurls forward. The first thing it encounters is the sharp edge of broken crust lacerating your ankle. The second is unbroken surface banging up your knee. The third point of contact is between your nose and the hard, cold crust.

How to avoid this ignominy? First, if you have a choice of skis, pick the longest, widest ones available. Spread the weight. Second, don't take along your 40-pound pack. Reduce the weight. Third, study the terrain. After an hour or so of observing subtle differences in the snow, you may be able to avoid the thinnest surface areas, thus keeping your body on top of the snow rather than in it. Your motto for crust: Weight Watchers.

CLEARING A FENCE

If you're skiing through farmland, sooner or later you're going to encounter a fence blocking your way. Probably sooner, and probably barbed wire. There are three ways through it. One is to use the gate. (For gate etiquette, see chapter 13.) Another is to duck under it, usually with a fellow skier holding up the bottom wire with his or her ski pole. The third, and most usual, way is to go over it. Here's how.

Ski right up to the fence and sidestep the final few feet. You're now standing parallel to the wires, with your left side next to them. Plant your left pole on the far side of the fence, your right pole next to your right leg. Balancing on your right foot, lift your left ski over the fence and set it down next to the pole. Lean on that pole as you bring your right ski up and over. The trick is to keep your skis parallel to each other and the fence.

Fig. 59a

Fig. 59a–b *Fence clearing*

Fig. 59b

BACKCOUNTRY SKI GEAR

In terms of gear, off-trail or backcountry skiing ideally calls for skis a bit wider than those designed for skiing in set tracks or racing. But "ideally" should not be confused with "gotta have." Under all but extreme conditions, you can have fun on in-track or racing skis in a park, a snowy pasture, or the A&P parking lot. It's the same with boots. Ideally, backcountry boots should offer more support and keep out more snow than those used for skiing set tracks. But if you slip gaiters over low boots, they'll be fine.

As for poles, I still say poles are poles—most of the time. But under exceptional circumstances, poles are more than poles. In steep country and in avalanche country, poles have to serve other functions as well. When you're spending a day or a week skiing up and down sides of mountains, you'll appreciate poles that expand and contract. It's much like raising and lowering the seat on your mountain bike—up for pedaling efficiency, down for safety and comfort. With expandable ski poles, you can do much the same thing. Keep them long for power on the flats and uphills; then shorten them for safety and comfort on the way down.

In avalanche country, the pole has a second, grimmer function. If your party is caught in a snow slide, you may need to use it to probe for missing skiers. For this, you use an avalanche probe, a long, narrow pole for poking deep into the snow. Some ski poles are made for this purpose; they easily drop their baskets and screw together to form a probe. Life-Link International of Jackson Hole, Wyoming, makes poles for this purpose, as do Back Country Access, Black Diamond, Leki, Ramer, and Smith.

AVALANCHE!

This is as good a time as any to talk about avalanches. The dictionary will tell you that an avalanche is a snow slide, but that doesn't begin to hint at its potential power. In New Zealand, my family and I used to ski at Round Hill, an alpine area set in the Southern Alps overlooking Lake Tekapo. We stayed at the Tekapo Ski Club hut, a substantial A-frame set well back from the mountain. The hut slept forty more or less comfortably. One fine morning in late winter, it got in the way of an avalanche. When the rumbling died, they say there was nothing left of the hut and its contents bigger than a matchstick. Even allowing for catastrophe's natural affinity for exaggeration, the place was totally and permanently demolished in a matter of seconds.

If a building can be destroyed by avalanche, what hope is there for people? Since people are considerably more mobile than buildings, there is considerable hope. The first and best advice for avalanche safety is to stay out of avalanche zones. To ski through known avalanche danger is the equivalent of building a house on the side of Mount Vesuvius. Either way, you're playing for deadly stakes.

And don't think avalanche country is limited to the North American Rockies or the New Zealand Alps. Any place with fairly steep slopes and heavy snow cover can be dangerous. Your best protection is to query knowledgeable locals about what's safe and what's not. Don't let embarrassment keep you from asking what could be a lifesaving question.

If you even think you may be skiing in an avalanche area, arrive prepared. Make sure you and your party are equipped with shovels, probes, avalanche cords, and transceivers—electronic beacons that can lead rescuers to a buried skier while he or she still has life and breath.

Arrive mentally prepared as well. Here are the bare-bones basics of what you should know before you go:

- Skiing across an unstable snowpack can set off a catastrophe for yourself and your companions. Slab avalanches—the kind where a whole section of snow breaks off and slips down the hill—are most often triggered by the victims themselves. The safest route through an avalanche zone is over the ridgeline. Next best is in the valley, as far from the slopes as you can get. The most dangerous route is down or across the avalanche path. That's when your skis could set off disaster.
- Avalanche danger runs high on steep slopes combined with sudden weather changes, new snow, deep snow, strong winds, rain, thaw, or warm and sunny days.
- Steep gullies and treeless slopes are potential avalanche routes. Especially avoid the most dangerous route—a broad, treeless slope funneling into a gully.
- If you see the snowpack crack or hear it settle (*whumph*!), you're in a danger zone. Get out! If you can create cracks or settles by disturbing the snow with your poles or skis, get out fast.
- If you absolutely must ski across an avalanche zone, make the crossing one skier at a time. This greatly increases your chances of rescue and survival. Before you cross, remove the wrist straps from your poles and the safety straps from your skis. Loosen your backpack so you can shuck it quickly. Put on gloves, hat, hood, and goggles; zip up your parka. Make sure all transceivers are in the "transmit" mode.
- Never ski alone.

If you are caught in an avalanche, you can do a number of things to increase your chance of survival. Here are some potential lifesavers:

- If you hear it coming and can't get out of the way, quickly discard your skis, poles, and pack.

- Yell like hell so your party can mark your (LSP) last seen point.
- When the avalanche hits, try to stay on top by swimming the breaststroke through the churning snow.
- When you feel the slide coming to a stop, cover your mouth and nose with one hand and raise the other as high as possible.
- Don't waste your breath (literally) by yelling unless you believe you're within inches of the surface and rescuers are nearby.
- Try to stay calm until help comes. (This is infinitely easier to say than do.)

To learn more about avalanches, read the short but technical book *The ABC of Avalanche Safety*, by E. R. LaChapelle, and watch the factual but terrifying video *Avalanche Awareness*, by Alliance Communications.

SKIING SNOWMOBILE TRAILS

A less dramatic danger to skiers lurks on snowmobile trails. Particularly on weekends, these highways through the wilderness are driven by powerful machines at speeds comparable to those on the Jersey Turnpike.

It's always dangerous when pedestrians and high-speed machines try to occupy the same space at the same time, and that's exactly the case when skiers and snowmobilers share trails. To minimize the danger, I suggest you do as I do:

- Don't ski snowmobile trails on weekends or holidays.
- Stop frequently to listen for the whine of motors. Be especially careful on hills and blind corners. As loud as snowmobiles usually sound, their noise can be muffled by earth and snow, and even the gentle *swoosh* of skis on snow can mask their sound.
- When you hear snowmobiles approaching, step well off the track until they pass.
- Wave and smile as they pass. In their dark coveralls, black helmets, and darkly tinted face shields, snowmobilers may look ominous, but they're not. Like you, they're people who have found a way to enjoy the outdoors in winter.

MOUNTAINEERING

One form of backcountry skiing that does require special gear is ski mountaineering. Whether trekking the European Alps or skiing hut to hut in the Colorado Rockies, you want heavy-duty gear on and beneath your feet. The ski of choice here is one with steel edges, enough strength to minimize the chance of breakage in a high and lonely place, and enough width to float through ultrachallenging conditions. Your boots should be high enough for extra ankle support and roomy enough to let you slip on an extra pair of socks if the weather turns bad. Bindings must not only be stout, but also give the lateral support that will safely take you down mountainsides with a heavy pack on your back.

Climbing skins, which are attached to the ski base, are a great aid to ski mountaineering. Originally made of sealskin, they are designed to grip hard on uphill climbs and slide slowly on downhill runs. Do you need skins? If you're taking long climbing treks, yes. Otherwise, no.

Today's skins are made of nylon or mohair. Nylon lasts longer; mohair glides farther. The two most widely used types of skins are stick-ons and strap-ons. Almost everyone prefers the stick-ons because they're easier to, well, stick on and take off. They adhere to the ski base by means of a glued inner surface. Though this can be messy and require an application of glue remover when you reach the top of the climb, skins save so much time and effort on the uphill that they're worth the hassle.

Most skiers remove the skins before a descent, but if the downhill is really steep and scary, you can leave them on and use them as highly effective brakes.

When you take a lunch break, keep the skins out of direct sunlight, or they may ice up when you begin the afternoon's ski. If you're camping out, take the skins off the skis at night to let them dry to prevent icing. Icing is, after dealing with glue, the worst thing about skins. One way to prevent or minimize it is to spray the skins with silicone before they hit the mush. If your skins get coated with pine needles, mud, grit, and other assorted schmutz, try cleaning them by spraying on a household cleaner like Fantastic.

What if you're caught at the foot of a mountain without skins? Here's a tip from backcountry expert and L. L. Bean adviser Phil Savignano: "Run a strip of duct tape down the base of your skis, and coat it with a wax that's too warm for the day. This will give you too much grip for gliding, but just right for climbing. When you've completed the climb, pull off the tape and enjoy the glide."

Another trick, advocated by Chris Townsend in *Wilderness Skiing and Winter Camping*, is to wrap a spare strap around the ski and use that as a makeshift snow gripper.

GAITERS AND BOOT COVERS

If you're planning to spend half a day or more on skis and off tracks, buy or sew a pair of gaiters, nylon tubes that start above the calf and end on the top of the boot. Their sole function is to keep snow and ice where they belong—far away from your skin.

If you're planning to spend a full day or more off-track, and there's a chance of cold weather, buy or sew a set of fuzzy acrylic boot covers. Their sole function is to keep your feet warm in cold weather.

BACKPACKS

For day trips, almost any backpack will do (if you can get away with it, a fanny pack will do best), but as treks grow longer and loads heavier, a made-for-skiing pack looks—and feels—more and more attractive. Here's what to look for:

- A good ski pack has padded shoulder straps for long-haul comfort.
- A narrow profile, front to back, is best because it keeps the weight close to your body. And if you're riding chairlifts or hopping out of helicopters, that narrow profile is less likely to get tangled in the machinery.
- Straps on opposite corners of the pack let you carry your skis diagonally when tramping through tundra in search of snow.
- A soft-lined pocket with a storm flap keeps sunglasses and cameras scratch-free and dry.
- A ski mountaineering pack has an exterior pocket or strap for an avalanche shovel and a loop for an ice ax.

What to avoid? Don't ski with a pack that has an external frame or copious side pockets. Both will be forever in your way.

Can you buy a pack that meets these requirements without taking out a second mortgage? Here are three leading models that sell for $150 or under: Life-Link Guide Pack, North Face Patrol Pack, and Vortex 2200.

When loading your pack, keep the heavy items low and close to your back. Anything else throws off your balance when you're skiing. And when you're skiing down a mountain, keep all straps cinched tight—you don't want loose cargo shifting from side to side as you try to stay upright on skinny skis.

Here are some packing tips from the late backcountry guide Allan Bard: "First, get rid of your stuff sacks. You can squash in much more gear if you just push your gear in, one item on top of another. Second, start the season wearing a light pack and work up as your muscles get used to carrying the weight. Third, to minimize pack movement, wear a sweater instead of a windbreaker."

WHAT TO PACK

Assuming you're on waxed skis, the first item to think of for that backpack is a wax kit. Backcountry expert Phil Savignano's wax kit consists of blue hard wax, special red wax, universal klister, scraper, synthetic cork, and baby powder. Baby powder? Experienced skiers sprinkle it abundantly over old klister to make removal with a scraper easier.

What else should go in your pack? In addition to carabiners, ice axes, crampons, and other extreme gear, the famous extreme skier Scot Schmidt carries mittens, neck gaiter, vest, sunscreen, Leatherman tool, flashlight, water bottle, spare pole baskets, shovel, climbing skins, and a lunch box.

And then there's the first-aid kit. This can range from a couple of Band-Aids and a few aspirin to a porto-clinic. Guide Allan Bard favored the latter and threw in equipment to repair broken skis, bindings, climbing skins, poles, packs, tents, and stoves. Here are a few of his key people-repair items: extra sweater or down jacket, small tarp, fire starter and pot, cloth Band-Aids, 2-inch-wide athletic tape, moleskin and gauze 4-by-4s, a 6-inch Ace bandage, scissors, tweezers, penlight, medication for pain, erythromycin for infection, Neosporin for skin wounds, Motrin for strains and sprains, Flagyl for giardiasis. Pepto-Bismol for jelly belly, oil of clove for toothache, and the wonder drug aspirin for just about everything. Always take along plenty of water; dehydration is the most common ski malady.

Here are some other items I take into the woods:

- Croakies—those nerdy looking cords that hold your glasses on, even when you execute a face plant into deep powder.
- Swiss army knife for skiers. Instead of a saw, it comes with a mini wax scraper and enough screwdriver blades to handle any emergency, real or imagined. L. L. Bean sells them.
- Safety light. I don't go into the woods without a flashing light snapped to my parka or snuggled in my pack. In the unlikely event that I'm separated from my party or get caught beneath a falling fir, searchers will have a good chance of finding me before the coyotes do. I use the Lite Tracker from Lightning Bug Enterprises (412-347-1993) because you can run over it with a pickup truck and it will still flash.
- Blister kit. The Spenco Blister Kit slips in a pocket and contains what you need to prevent and treat blisters: dressings, blister pads, and strips of adhesive knit.
- Hand warmers, extra hat and ear jock, extra gloves or mittens. Even if I'm warm, someone else may get cold.
- Waterproof matches. Just in case.

PHOTOGRAPHY IN THE SNOWY WORLD

Effin Older, my wife, is a writer and photographer whose shots have appeared in most of the major ski magazines. Effin has shot on snow in Scotland, Iceland, Newfoundland, and a lot of other lands. She offers some advice on photography on your ski trips:

"Ski photography is different from other photography in several important ways: First, cold drains camera batteries quickly. Electronic cameras can freeze up in the middle of a shoot. Always carry extra batteries. I carry mine in a small pouch around my neck, inside my jacket, where my body heat keeps them warm. When things get really cold, I also keep a hand warmer next to my camera to keep the shutter from freezing.

"Second, you need to be able to move freely and quickly while skiing in terrain that includes cliffs, chutes, canyons, crannies, and couloirs. I usually ski with a padded fanny pack that holds one camera and six rolls of film. I can easily swing it around when I want to stop for a shot. If I need two cameras, extra lenses, flash, and monopod, I use a roomier zippered backpack made by Tamrac.

"Another challenge is getting the correct exposure, which can be pretty tricky when shooting skiers against a background of snow. Underexposure is the most common mistake when taking ski pictures. If I'm using ISO 100 film on a bright, sunny day, I set my shutter speed at 500 and my lens between f/8 and f/11. This gives me white snow, blue sky, and brightly colored skiers."

Winter's Diary: December 20

Finders Keepers. During the shortened days of December, we are yet again cross-country skiing in the fields behind our little home. There are five of us this day—Effin, Marsha, me, and a pair of snow-loving dogs. It's a brilliant winter afternoon. The sun is bright in the sky, the snow is white on the ground, and a few flakes are languidly falling, their angles catching the sun and sparkling like diamonds in the clear country air.

We've just crossed the road and are skiing up a short rise, where the view in all directions is mountain peaks and distant woods. Effin spots it first. She stops and points. "What's that?"

Marsha and I ski over to a white, plastic rectangle lying half buried in the snow. It's about the size of small shoebox and has a long line attached to it. The line is stretched taut and disappears beneath the snow a few feet away.

Marsha asks the same question: "What is it?"

Suddenly I know. "It's an animal trap. Bloody old Ronald must have set it here. What's the matter with him, laying a trap where skiers and dogs are sure to get caught in it?"

Effin calls the dogs and skis some distance away from the infernal instrument. Marsha and I approach it.

I'm of two minds. I don't care for animal traps of any kind, and this one is set in a place that could be a real danger to people and pets. On the other hand, Ronald counts on traps to make his spending money. His job at the mill covers little more than the basics. And as for my feelings about traps, they're a distinctly minority view in this country area. A lot of my neighbors run trap lines for muskrat, fox, or any other fur-bearing critter that will take the bait.

Despite my ready identification of the contraption, it doesn't look like any trap I've seen before. It's plastic, not steel, and there are no sharp teeth visible. But there is a rectangular hole at the top that reminds me of a feeder in a psychology department rat cage. And on the side that is sticking out of the snow, I can read the words "Manufactured in Canada."

In Canada. Well, that confirms it. Canadians are famous trappers, and they've obviously come up with a better trap. White plastic on white snow—the animals don't stand a chance against this cunning Canadian technology.

And now these Canadians are exporting their improved animal trap to the United States. Very nice. I suppose this is their revenge for our sending them a little acid rain.

I make up my mind. "We've got to set it off."

Effin holds the dogs. Marsha and I ski closer. She pokes the thing with her ski pole a few times. Nothing happens.

"Stand back!" I say. "I'll do it." I take a deep breath and swing my pole in a reverse uppercut. *Thwack*! Something snaps in the top of the trap. "I think I got it!" I shout. "Let's go look."

Effin releases the dogs and skis over, muttering about anyone who would set traps where dogs could get into them.

With my ski pole, I tentatively turn the contraption on its side. In large blue letters, it says, "AVIS."

Avis? Is this a rental trap? I don't know—the message beneath "AVIS" is all in French. I turn the box over, still using my ski pole to make sure it doesn't snap me.

The message on the other side is in English. Silently, we read it together:

> NOTICE TO FINDER: This is a weather instrument known as a "Radiosonde." It was used for measuring the air temperature, pressure and humidity at various heights above the ground. It was carried aloft by a balloon released by the Atmospheric Environment Service–Canada.
>
> During the observation, the radiosonde operated as a radio transmitter which was tracked by a special radio receiver at the ground stations. This radiosonde has now served its purpose and it is not economical to repair it. THE FINDER IS REQUESTED NOT TO RETURN IT. The finder is warned that the battery in the clear plastic bag contains a corrosive liquid which may cause injury to the clothing or skin.

The three of us look at each other. I grab the cord and follow it through the snow. I have to go 50 feet before I find the orange parachute attached to the other end. All that's left of the weather balloon is a 6-inch segment of thick rubber.

We look at each other again and begin to laugh and laugh. The dogs start to bark happily. We gather the trap–trick weather station, its antenna cord, parachute, and the remains of the balloon. This is just the thing for Marsha's son to take to school for show-and-tell.

8

Touring Centers

For years I skied only in fields and woods, down snow-covered roads, and occasionally through city streets. I can't remember when I first became aware that there were such things as ski touring centers, but I well remember my first visit to one. It was the Craftsbury Outdoor Center in northern Vermont.

For the past few weeks, I'd been breaking trail through heavy snow in and around my Vermont home. One day I decided to try this Craftsbury place I'd been hearing about. So up I drove.

Whoa! Other people on skis! A warming hut! Hot soup for sale! Actual marked trails and even a trail map! All this was radical enough, but what really caught my attention was when I set my skis in the grooves and pushed off. My, oh my—no wonder there were so many people here! This was the most effortless skiing I'd ever experienced. The track kept my gliding ski steady and kept me moving in the right direction. My glide seemed to go on forever. And the snow was groomed to be fast and fabulous. Ohhh, so this was what it was about!

Since that happy day, I've tried track skiing from Nevada to Newfoundland. With few exceptions, I've enjoyed that same experience—speed without effort, glide without wobble. Plus the companionship of other skiers. And a few bonuses as well, such as a warm room, hot soup, flush toilets—the basic amenities. Another is a rental shop—a chance to try before you buy into a new sport. For two- or three-day-a-year skiers, especially those who live in digs where storage space is short, renting may be a better option than buying, even after you've discovered that you love the sport.

A third bonus available at touring centers is the ski instructor. It's a good idea to take a lesson now and then. Good lessons (they're not all like the one I described earlier) get you started in the right direction and keep you advancing.

Fig. 60 *A ski lesson*

Excuse me, Jules.

Yes?

Have you taken many lessons?

Uh, no, not really.

Well?

When I started cross-country skiing, as far as I knew, there were no lessons. By the time I got around to taking them, I was reasonably set in my ways. But I've learned two things from the few lessons I've taken. One is that to ski "right" (and by that I mean most efficiently and skillfully), I'd have to unlearn many of the things I've taught myself. The second is that good lessons help speed up the learning process. So, do I take them? Not very often. Do I recommend them? Indeed, I do. You needn't be as pigheaded as I am.

Jonathan Wiesel, ski journalist and author of *Cross-Country Ski Vacations*, consultant in ski-area planning, and international trips coordinator for Off the Beaten Path Tours (800-445-2995), who has also put in time as an instructor, guide, groomer, and ski patroller, offers the following on ski lessons:

"It is possible to appreciate cross-country skiing without knowing how and when to snowplow, step turn, or stretch out into the long, graceful diagonal stride that eats up the kilometers. But walking on skis—which is what most of us do—gives only a taste of winter's rapture. Hacking around on your own supplies the shortcake but no strawberries and cream.

"Professional instruction can transform plod into glide, boredom into ecstasy. The range of techniques is astonishing—not just classic style, but also ski-skating and more types of turns than you can accomplish on alpine equipment.

"It's tempting to assume you can absorb the basics in a couple of hours on a golf course under the tutelage of a friend or sweetheart. This approach promises not only nervous prostration and a wet fundament, but also shattered relationships.

"Professional Ski Instructors of America (PSIA) and Canadian Association of Nordic Ski Instructors (CANSI) train their people to communicate effectively. Their aims are to create efficiency, diversity, and entertainment so that skiers will learn a half dozen ways to ski the flats or ascend a hill—everything from herringboning to gliding straight up. Most importantly, these specialists can teach you to control those boards downhill, using anything from the dependable traverse to a dashing skate turn.

"It's easiest and most comfortable to learn at a cross-country area with set trails. If there's a choice, women tend to be better guides than men, with greater patience, less ego, more emphasis on elegance than strength.

"Finally, instruction coupled with only a couple of days' practice each winter won't really hone your skills. Figure on a dozen outings a year to make true progress and transform mere exercise into a banquet of the senses."

I'd also recommend that if you're tentative about trying cross-country skiing, spend your first days with the sport at a touring center. Between the rental skis, the places to come out of the cold, the lessons, and the set tracks, it should increase the chances that you'll fall in love with skiing. But before you go, you should know something about touring-center etiquette. Here are the rules:

- Don't walk on trails—they're for skis only. Your bootprints become icy holes in what was a pristine track.
- Ski to the right; pass on the left.
- Holler "Track!" when you want to pass another skier. Then add the phrase "On your left," just to make sure the message is clear.
- If you meet another skier in a single track, step aside if you're going uphill and she is coming downhill. Getting out of a track while speeding downhill isn't easy.
- If you're both on the level, step aside anyway.
- If you're skating, don't skate through classic set tracks. It royally screws them up by breaking down their walls.

- If you fall, get up and out of the track as quickly as you can. Don't panic, but don't sit there, either.
- You get extra politeness points if you fill in the hole you made when you fell.
- Leave the dog at home. Keep those trails white!
- Pay your trail fee. That's what covers the cost of trail maintenance and grooming. Even though it may be easy to sneak onto trails, resist the temptation.

What's involved in grooming? There aren't many people who know more about grooming than John Tidd, president of Tidd Tech Ltd., Vermont-based "purveyors of fine implements for cross-country trail grooming." Here's Tidd on grooming:

"Skiers often ask what makes those little ruts in the snow. They're often surprised to find out that they are mechanically set by machines costing up to $200,000. Larger ski areas groom their trails using the same snow cats you see grooming alpine ski hills. The only difference is that the final grooming implement is a track setter that molds tracks into the snow. Smaller ski areas use snowmobiles to drag a variety of implements to do the same thing.

"Whether the machinery is big or small, the task of grooming a ski trail involves several processes. First, new snow must be packed down to a firm, flat surface that will support the skier. For skating, this is often enough, but for classical striding, ski tracks must be molded into the surface. When the snow becomes too hard from traffic or freeze-thaw weather patterns, the snow must be renovated. This means tilling, grinding, or slicing the snow into fine granules, thus restoring the surface to a skiable texture. Then the tracks can be set again in the loose, granular snow.

"Grooming trails for cross-country skiing is a time-consuming and expensive operation. It requires many hours of machine time, often late at night in the worst weather. Grooming costs are a major portion of the trail fees charged by the areas. But it's well worth the expense when you can ski a perfect carpet of freshly groomed snow on a crisp winter day."

GETTING LOST

That perfect-carpet day can be seriously impaired if you can't figure out where you are. You figure out where you are by maps and signs. Unfortunately, an awful lot of touring centers don't take their signage seriously. You come to a trail intersection and don't know whether to turn left or right, whether you're heading back to the lodge or into the Fire Swamp. Since getting lost in winter can have grave consequences, I consider this a major failing . . . and one that area owners apparently don't consider a high priority.

SHAMELESS PROMOTION, CANADIAN-STYLE

Toni Scheier of Cross Country Canada offers ten irresistible reasons to ski the Maple Leaf:

1. Good snow, long season.
2. 2.6 million Canadian skiers can't be wrong.
3. The hot tub at Putnam Station Hotel, Silver Star, British Columbia. Ski from the hotel to the trails at Silver Star Mountain Resort.
4. The Canmore Nordic Centre, Canmore, Alberta, host site of the 1988 Olympic races and home of the National Ski Team.
5. The Lappe Nordic Ski Centre, a bit of Finland in North America, just on the edge of Thunder Bay Ontario, site of the 1995 Nordic World Ski Championships. Stay at the Airlane Hotel, the Athletes' Village for the Worlds (maybe you can stay in Bjorn Daehlie's old room).
6. Great skiing just north of Toronto in southern Ontario. Hardwood Hills even has artificial snow for mild winters, and nearby Duntroon Highlands hosts many National and International events.
7. Gatineau Park in Ottawa/Hull has hundreds of kilometers of trails for all levels of skiers.
8. Mont-Ste.-Anne, Quebec, has superb cross-country trails with a French ambience.
9. There are four hundred ski clubs from the Yukon to Newfoundland.
10. http://canada.x-c.com

So what can you do to reduce the risk of getting lost? Study the big trail map at the warming hut, ask for a small map to take with you, and take the sign-in seriously. The sign-in is writing your name, the time, and the trails you're expecting to ski in the book they hand you when you pay your trail fee.

Just in case you still get lost, come prepared. Because you're on groomed trails, it's easy to get lax about basic safety procedures. That's just what we did on a sunny Saturday afternoon. We were only skiing for an hour, we told ourselves. And we knew the trails pretty well. So we took no food, no water, no map, no Band-Aids, no extra clothing of any kind. And of course, we got lost. In a snowstorm. With too little food in our stomachs.

The hour turned into three hours. The 5 kilometers turned into more like 35. We limped back in the dark, tired, wet, hungry, dehydrated, disgusted, and with blistered heels. At least we'd brought our hats. Just not our brains.

Even if you're skiing familiar territory—bring both.

SKIING ON AND OFF A BUDGET

Talking to hearty, bearded cross-country types, you may get the impression that you have to love sleeping in snowbanks to really enjoy cross-country skiing. *Mais non*! It is true that rude shelters, log huts, and dormlike ski lodges abound in the cross-country world, but it's also true that some of the most luxurious resorts on the continent offer nordic skiing as well. Here's a small sample:

At Dixville Notch, New Hampshire, the Balsams Grand Resort Hotel has specialized in extravagant accommodations for well over a century. In addition to its own lift-served mountain, the Balsams maintains more than 150 kilometers of cross-country trails. One state west, the Equinox in Manchester, Vermont, and Topnotch Resort in Stowe are two of the most deluxe spa resorts in the Green Mountain State, and both are also famous for their cross-country skiing.

Continue moving west, and halfway between Montreal and Ottawa you'll come to the 210-room Le Chateau Montebello, billed as the world's biggest log building; it's not only luxurious, it's a major center for skinny skiing. Cross the border and head next to northern Michigan and the Grand Traverse Resort, the Midwest's biggest resort complex. Then, drop down to Edwards, Colorado, and ski Cordillera, a slightly miniaturized Xanadu with a Euro-western flavor and all the class that money can buy. Still in Colorado, 50 lucky people at a time get to ski Irwin Lodge and its more than 600 inches of snow on more than 2,000 acres of national forest. Farther west and across the border again, you're at Banff, Jasper, and Lake Louise Hotel, gems of the Canadian Rockies . . . and a haven for prosperous cross-country skiers.

What's it like to stay at one of these ski palaces? Here was my introduction to Cordillera:

When I walked through the massive front door and into the maple-paneled lobby, a smiling concierge said, "You must be exhausted after your flight and drive. We've arranged a massage for you whenever you're ready."

Her words saddened me. I suddenly realized that I'd lived my whole life, and nobody had ever cared enough about how exhausted I felt after a fifty-minute flight and two-hour drive to offer me a massage. Thanks a lot, Mom!

Winter's Diary: January 10

Ten. Today is the Mona Lisa of ski days. It's the Empire State Building, the perfectly steamed Maine lobster, the Eine Kleine Nacht Musik, *the Princess Bride*, the *Grapes of Wrath*. Ski day–wise, it's a ten out of ten.

Yes, on the tenth day of January, with the thermometer reading 10 degrees, the skiing is a perfect ten. For the past two or three nights we've had a light drop of snow. Although the sun is bright in the cloudless cobalt sky, the temperature has remained cold enough to keep the snow in a state of pristine lightness. We're skiing powder, and we're out before the snowmobiles, before any other skiers, even before the dogs have tracked it. We're pioneering.

What a feeling! We g-l-l-lide down the hill, skis hi-s-s-sing through the forgiving snow. We s-l-l-lide across the swamp, skimming over the icy water of early winter, over the frozen muck below that, through 6 inches of fluffy new snow.

Grinning and panting, we run along the level bottom of Mike Rice's field, through gentle drifts a foot deep. Each step feels for all the world as though we're running in slow motion—leaping forward, then sinking slowly into the powder toward a welcoming earth.

On the bottom I'm wearing long johns and nylon shell pants; on top, a T-shirt, flannel shirt, and light wool sweater. Though it's only 10 degrees, I'm warm and, on uphill climbs, downright hot.

This is what skiing is all about. This is what living in Vermont is all about.

In my room overlooking most of northern Colorado, I changed into a fluffy, white Cordillera bathrobe; strolled down the broad, stone steps past a suit of armor; took a moment to gaze appreciatively at the long, handsome indoor pool; and entered the steam room. There I sat until a beautiful young woman with a French accent called my name. "I am Florence," she said. "Pleaze follow me."

Still think you have to sleep in a snowbank?

9

Telemarking

Telemarking was the invention of Sondre Norheim, a skiing farmer from Morgedal, in the Telemark region of Norway. At a competition in 1868, he astounded the crowd by first jumping 76 feet, then capping it with a graceful turning stop. That finale was the start of what came to be known as telemarking.

Norheim's jumping and turning skills only partially accounted for his stellar performance; his innovating skills accounted for the rest. Norheim built his own skis, and he built them shorter and lighter than those of his competitors. His heel bindings, which he made from twisted birch roots, gave him an edge in stability. Norheim went on to pioneer the parallel turn and an awkward but efficient climbing technique, the herringbone. So he invented a new ski, a new binding, two new turns, and a new way of climbing hills. Not bad for a farmer from the sticks.

Twenty years later, another Norwegian, Fridtjof Nansen, adapted Norheim's techniques for his forty-day, 320-mile trek across Greenland. Nansen's book about his journey was translated into many languages and ignited a new interest in skiing as recreation. It also inspired adventurous snow dwellers to design lighter, shorter skis than the long boards they'd inherited from their parents.

In the mountains of Colorado and Nevada, miners used long skis and telemark turns for recreation as well as transportation, as did city-dwelling Canadians. By the turn of the century, Montrealers were happily telemarking down the slopes of Mont Royal in the heart of the city.

Eventually, improved skis, boots, and bindings made alpine turning easier, and gradually the telemark turn went the way of Meergan straps and Cubco bindings—out of use and into ski history. With Austrians favoring fixed heels and steel edges, and Norwegians leaning toward free heels and skinny skis, telemarking fell into the growing crevasse between. It all but disappeared.

But in the early 1970s, telemarkers began reappearing at a number of western ski areas, especially the wild and woolly Crested Butte, Colorado. A Crested Butte ski writer named Rick Borkovek started publishing articles about the technique, and pretty soon it was back in force. After decades of disuse, a telemark race was held in 1974, not in Norway, but in Breckenridge, Colorado.

Today telemarkers learn their turns at alpine ski areas all over North America. They're easy to spot—they're the ones sinking to one knee, as if in prayer, at every turn. They're the ones with free heels, funny-looking Peruvian hats, and gorilla thighs.

You may ask this: If the alpine ski industry has spent 800 kazillion dollars designing equipment to make skiing easier, why go back to an ancient technique that's guaranteed to make it harder? It's a fair question with at least two answers.

First, you can do things on telemarks that you can't do on alpine skis. You can ski uphill. You can shoulder your relatively light skis and hike to a peak in your relatively flexible boots. You can ski cross-country trails and logging roads. You can leave behind the often-crowded, usually expensive world of the ski resort.

Fig. 61 *Isa Oehry telemarking*

Second, not everybody likes things easy. When Isa Oehry left Liechtenstein for Vermont, she quickly found herself bored on our comparatively tame mountains. "So I took up telemarking, and all of a sudden I was having fun again." Isa went on to be a world leader in telemark racing.

Like snowboarding and snowshoeing, telemarking provides another way to enjoy the world in winter. Here's how to start. Rather, here's where to start. Start in your living room. Start by putting on sneakers and sweatpants and lowering yourself into the telemark position. Put your left leg a foot or two in front of the right, divide your weight more or less evenly between them, then sink down toward the floor. Hold the position. Switch legs and do it again. Switch legs and do it again. Switch legs and do it again.

What you're doing is teaching your body the position so that when it's time to hit the slopes, it will feel fine and natural, not awkward and uncomfortable. You're also building up your leg muscles.

Once you've mastered the living room, move on . . . to the gas station while you're filling up your car, to the phone booth while you're in voice-mail jail, to the IGA while you're standing in the world's longest checkout line. Practice the telemark position (Fig. 62).

Fig. 62 *The telemark position*

And now it's time to practice it on skis. Pick a gentle slope, not a chute, and move slowly, not at speed. Ski down or across the hill, and as you're skiing, sink into the telemark position. Switch legs and do it again. Switch legs and do it again. Switch legs and do it again. Only after you feel secure with that movement should you add turning to the maneuver.

Turning? That's what telemarking's about, remember?

In 1988 Mike Miller looked into telemark skiing classes and didn't like what he saw. "I quickly realized that none of the teaching methods worked. They were either too complicated or required more than one lesson just to learn how to make a simple turn. I thought, there just has to be a better way to teach this stuff."

He set out to find it. After considerable trial and error, Miller came up with five steps that take a skier from pure novice to basic telemarker in one two-hour lesson. In his words, "We want people to learn fast and have fun. In two hours you'll be able to make strong, confident telemark turns."

Now that is quite a challenge—and one I decided to accept. Since I had never been on tele skis and was not now, nor had I ever been, a super-jock, I figured I was as good a test case as any.

So I showed up at Miller's Telemark Ski School at Killington's Sunrise Base Lodge one foggy morning in February. They fitted me with skis and

Fig. 63 *Wedge*

boots, then introduced me to my instructor, Isa Oehry from Liechtenstein (which she pronounces "Lee-ickkk-ten-schtine"). Because I already knew how to downhill ski, Isa took me up the chairlift to the top of a long, reasonably gentle trail. The lesson began as soon as we got off.

Step one of the Miller Method is—surprisingly—getting into a basic wedge turn (Fig. 63). While I got the feel of turning on free-heel skis, Isa observed my stance, posture, and degree of (dis)comfort. When she was satisfied that I was making solid wedge turns, we went on to step two.

Fig. 64 *Heel lift between turns*

Now she had me briefly raise my uphill heel (the one closest to the top of the slope) during the traverse between turns (Fig. 64). I found this a lot harder than it looked and stomped it back down after a microsecond. But under her patient guidance, I soon became comfortable with this new—and as yet pointless—trick.

For the third step, she instructed me to raise the heel at the beginning of the traverse and hold it until I started the next turn. While I practiced, she worked with me on balance and body position. I was still no whiz, but I was beginning to feel more comfortable with the telemark skis' relative lack of stability.

The fourth step was to start the heel lift still earlier—halfway through the turn before the traverse (Fig. 65). I was still initiating the turn with both heels down but was now slowly working the lift into the turning process. Soon I had the uphill heel more or less raised all the time. More or less. Less. But I was beginning to get the feel of it. And I was beginning to see—actually, to feel—the point of all this heel raising. It was gradually working me into the telemark stance.

Fig. 65 *Heel lift in turn*

Fig. 66 *Leading uphill ski*

When I got the feel enough to approximate a steady-state heel lift, Isa moved me into the fifth and final step, pushing the uphill ski into the lead (Fig. 66). From there it was a short step from my wedged A-frame turns to parallel telemarking. I couldn't do this with ease, and certainly not with any grace, but I could do it.

While I wasn't about to win any contests for speed or looks, I could now change direction on all but the steepest parts of the trail. I felt confident enough to actually start enjoying myself. And I did make it to the bottom of the mountain on free-heel skis, using new turning techniques. Total time elapsed: one hour, twenty minutes. Huzzah!

For novices as well as alpine skiers, learning to telemark does not come naturally. There seems to be so much to think about—Which foot gets the weight? Which ski slides forward?—that you can end up feeling like the centipede trying to remember which leg to move next. Expect initial awkwardness; you won't be disappointed.

But here's something simple to hold on to. Turns come when you weight your front big toe and rear little toe. Front big, rear little. Try it.

Fig. 67a

Fig. 67b

Fig. 67a–d *Wedge to parallel telemarking*

Fig. 67c

Fig. 67d

So the Miller Method works. The next question is, how come? I think I know the answer.

First, Miller's analysis of the telemark learning process is a good one, and the five steps are well designed. Second, classes are small—no more than three in a class, not ten or twenty. And third, he chooses his teachers carefully. Not only was Isa patient, kind, and knowledgeable, she was also a member of the U.S. National Telemark Team and one of the fastest telemarkers in the world. Miller himself is a lifetime skier and former racing coach.

Mike Miller offers the following contrarian advice: "My ski school is famous for teaching skiers how to make strong, confident telemark turns in just two hours. But what excites me even more is that they learn how to telemark ski the way it was meant to be—with leather boots. What is the point of telemarking in all-plastic boots? What is the difference between the turns skiers make in those boots versus alpine boots? None! Plastic is giving skiers a cheap imitation of what telemark skiing truly is—skill, strength, and leather.

"If you want to learn how to telemark, here is my advice. First, rent good telemark boots that are all leather and relatively new. Second, make sure your instructor also wears leather boots. I promise you will be happier in the long run, because you will actually be earning the turns. And it is awesome!"

THE RANDONÉE ALTERNATIVE

Telemarking is but one way to conquer steep mountain slopes. An alternative, more popular in Europe than North America, is randonée. Randonée equipment is modified alpine gear—heavy plastic boots, razor-edged skis, stratospheric prices. The major difference is in the binding, which lets you raise your heel for the trek up and lock it to the ski for the ride down. If you already own alpine equipment, you can avoid buying all new gear by buying a climbing adapter like the Alpine Trekker, which you use on the way up and stow on the way down.

Telemark or randonée—which one's for you? According to mountain expert John Dostal, "On steep terrain or junky snow, most alpine skiers will feel more confident with a randonée rig. But free-heel gear is easier on your feet and thighs when skiing on trails or moderate backcountry terrain, while offering enough support for scaling the heights. And remember this—it's simply not necessary to make thigh-straining genuflections of the telemark turn to ski in the backcountry on free-heel gear. Parallels work just fine, especially when you're wearing the recently developed plastic free-heel boots."

SAFETY

Cross-country skiing has long been considered a particularly safe sport. But telemarking may prove an exception to that cheering assumption. A study is now under way to determine just how safe telemarking really is, and while the final results are not yet in, the preliminary findings aren't entirely reassuring.

The study is being conducted in Seattle by physician and skier Mike Tuggy. Here's what he's found so far:

- The telemark injury rate is about one in one hundred skier days, or roughly one injury every three to five years. That's slightly higher than the rate for alpine skiers, but the severity of the injuries is considerably lower.
- The most frequently injured part of the body is the knee, followed by the thumb and ankle.
- Telemarkers most frequently injure themselves when they're hungry—between eleven and noon and again between two and four.
- Roughly half the injuries occur on the steep terrain at downhill resorts, and half on the uneven snow in the backcountry.

By the way, you can participate in this study. Contact Dr. Mike Tuggy, Swedish Family Medicine, 1401 Madison St., Suite 100, Seattle, WA 98104-1338, (206) 386-6054 or 6281. Or contact him on the Web at http://weber.u.washington.edu/~mtuggy/sfm/telepag2.htm.

As a result of his pioneering, ongoing study, Dr. Tuggy has come up with a number of other observations about injuries in cross-country and telemark skiing. And he's reached some conclusions about exercise and injury prevention.

Cross-country skiers are subject to several common injuries—falls involving the shoulder, wrist, and ankle or overuse injuries of the lower leg. Wrist sprains, shoulder dislocations, and ankle sprains are the major injuries that are likely to limit a skier during any given season. Fortunately, these injuries usually occur at rates of less than four per thousand days of skiing.

The best preventive measures you can take to reduce the risk of injury are to strengthen the shoulder girdle and lower leg muscle groups with focused high-intensity strengthening exercises. The simple push-up combined with butterfly exercises with dumbbells, practiced three times a week in sets of twenty (or until the muscles are fatigued), will provide greater stability in the event of a fall. The ankle is best strengthened using single-leg toe raises on a step and isometric ankle exercises. To do those exercises, use your ankle muscle to twist your foot up, first left, then right. While you're twisting, press your hand against the foot to resist its movement.

The telemark skier is more likely to sustain knee and thumb injuries as well as ankle injuries. The injury rate for telemark skiers is about ten per thousand days of skiing. Because of the higher speeds with their falls, telemark knee injuries often include significant ligament sprains. Plastic boots do not appear to increase the risk of injury and, in fact, may reduce it slightly.

Winter's Diary: January 22

Un-Presidential. We're spending President's Day in the capital—the Canadian capital. We're here for Winterlude, the region's celebration of its longest and strongest season—winter. A major part of that celebration is cross-country skiing. In fact, the high point of Winterlude is the prestigious international ski race the Keskinada Lopet. The Keskinada is 50 kilometers of skating up and down hills, across Meech Lake, through checkpoints and food stations manned by eager volunteers shouting, "*L'eau*! Water! *L'eau*! Water!"

Suddenly, Ottawa looks like Oslo, with ski racks on every other car and skinny skis crowding the corner of every other office. Elite skiers from all over the globe compete in the race, but just behind them in the massed start are less-than-elite skiers of every ilk: fat and thin, old and young, fiercely competitive and out for a long plod through the park. They wear everything from Lycra and epoxy to knickers and Norwegian wood. When we watch two thousand of them take off at once, it's hard to believe we're in North America. And even harder to wipe the grins off our faces and the tears from our eyes. To see so many people having so much fun on skinny skis . . . oh, my!

Aggressive strengthening exercises like lunges and other quadriceps exercises will help you respond more quickly to rapid shifts in balance. And because most serious knee injuries arise from falls where the skier pitches back over the tails of the skis, try to keep your upper body forward in an aggressive stance if a fall is imminent. To reduce the likelihood of shoulder dislocation, use the same upper-body training recommended above for cross-country skiers.

Overall, injuries in both sports are more common among beginners than among experienced skiers. Proper training and technique, especially early in the development of skiing skills, will lead to many years of enjoyable free-heel skiing.

10

Waxing

Let's start with the bad news: Even if you bought waxless skis, you're going to have to know something about wax. And even if you bought waxless skating skis, you're going to have to know something about wax.

The good news is—well, there's double good news. First, if you bought waxless skis, you don't need to know a whole lot about wax. Second, waxing is actually a lot of fun. It's time-consuming, but it's satisfying. What's more, the deeper you delve into the intricacies of wax, the more satisfying it becomes. Not only can you instantly (and literally) apply this knowledge, but you also can feel the results of your new learning in the first three strides. If your skis grip like glue on the kick and slip like a dolphin through the glide, you know you got it right.

But before we start our glide into waxes and waxing, you need to know something about snow and physics.

As Snowflake Bentley, the self-taught Vermont scientist, discovered, snowflakes are intricate, elegant hexagons, full of lacy patterns hung on sharp points. At least that's how they look as they fall from the sky. But after they've lain around for a couple of days, their looks undergo a sharp decline. The intricate patterns collapse. The sharp points dull. Depending on conditions, the hexagon becomes a blunt and pointless ball or, worse, a blob. They're just no fun anymore.

Unless you're a skier. Then you'll discover that these rounded, dulled, blobified flakes create a much faster surface than their fresh, pointy cousins. Because points and patterns create friction, they catch on ski bottoms. But balls, like ball bearings, let skis slide on by. Fresh powder feels like cotton gauze; old snow, under the right conditions, feels like silk. Old snow under the wrong conditions, however, feels like ice. It *is* ice. Under other wrong conditions, it's slush or breakable crust or thick crud. Worry not; you can wax for these conditions, too. But before we talk about how, let's briefly light on everyone's favorite high school subject—physics.

When a ski crosses snow, it creates friction. That friction creates heat. And that heat melts a thin layer of snow under the ski. Friction, heat, melt. That melted snow, in the form of water droplets, lubricates the contact point between ski and snow and thus reduces the friction between them. And that's what allows your moving ski to glide instead of jerking painfully along. A moving ski glides, but a stationary ski grips. It's that grip that allows you to kick off and start your next stride.

What sits between ski and snow, and what allows the glide and the grip, is wax. Two waxes: glide wax and grip wax.

GLIDE WAX

Ah, but what about waxless skis? Their grip comes from raised patterning on the ski's kick zone, the part that extends a foot or so fore and a few inches aft of your boot. Even on waxless skis, however, the glide still relies on wax, on what's appropriately called *glide wax*. That's one reason even owners of waxless skis should know about it. The other reason is that wax also protects the ski from scraping by rocks and roots and, in summer, from oxidation by air and the sun. Glide wax makes skis last longer.

Everyone's first question is, then why are they called waxless? Because you don't apply kick wax.

Everyone's second question is, if you own waxless skis, should you wax the kick zone as well as the glide zone? This is an area of controversy, but here's my take for it: If your skis are chemically treated, not patterned, don't wax the kick zone. If they're patterned (and this is much more likely), wax the entire base of the ski for protection.

There are five ways to apply wax. The fastest is to smear NOTwax on and go skiing. NOTwax is a wax substitute that's remarkably long lasting, but it's only for skis with sintered bases. NOTwax can't be used on cheaper, extruded bases. The fastest for extruded bases is to squirt liquid wax (F4 is the best-known brand) onto the base, wait a few minutes, lightly buff it, and go skiing. The most common way to wax is to take a tube or canister of solid wax, rub it on the base, wait a few minutes, then smooth it out and work it in with a waxing cork. The most traditional way to wax is to heat the wax with a clothing iron or a made-for-waxing iron, drip it onto the skis, iron the wax dots in, scrape off the excess, brush it smooth (a step nonracers and nonperfectionists can easily skip), wait a few minutes, and then go skiing. The most expensive method is to take your skis to a ski shop and let them do it for you.

Me, I'm an ironer. I like the smell of wax, I like the process of waxing, and even though I've pretty much switched to waxless skis, I keep them

Fig. 68 *Applying F4 wax on the trail*

smooth and protected with glide wax. If my skis start sticking on the trail, I apply some NOTwax and resume gliding.

Here's the best way to wax skis by the traditional ironed-on method. In a heated but well-ventilated workroom, set a room-temperature ski on a pair of ski vises. (If you try waxing a cold ski you've just brought in, you'll be waxing on water. Wait for the condensation to evaporate.) Start by cleaning the bottoms of your skis with a wax remover. Bear in mind that many wax removers, particularly the older types, are not only combustible, but are probably hard on lungs as well. So don't smoke around them (don't smoke at all), and keep the ventilation going.

Heat your iron to 130 degrees Celsius (that's 266 degrees Fahrenheit). An overheated iron can burn a ski's base, which is something you want to avoid. But if your iron doesn't have a temperature gauge, how do you know when it's overheated? If it smokes, it's too hot. Turn it down to the lowest setting and keep it there. Now, holding the stick or block of wax against the iron, let little drops of wax drip over the part of the base you intend to wax. Then iron it in, spreading the wax drops over the entire area you want to cover.

When it dries, scrape the excess off with a piece of flat plastic, and scoop it out of the groove with a plastic spoon. Better still, use an inexpensive plastic ski scraper, available at any ski shop. Ideally, let the skis cool at room temperature for forty-five minutes before scraping in order to let the wax set. If you've waxed dirty skis, however, begin scraping immediately, while the wax is still molten; you'll take off the dirt along with the excess wax.

How much wax is excess? Figure to remove up to 90 percent of the wax you just ironed in. Glide wax is intended to penetrate the base, not sit on its surface. If you're a racer or perfectionist (I'm neither), after waxing, brush the bases with brushes (short-bristle copper brush for wet snow and nylon or horsehair for dry), then buff them with a Fibertex pad. Chore Girl pads work fine.

There are two things you can do before waxing to improve your skis' performance. A flat ski is a fast ski. Hold a metal scraper at several points along the ski bottom. If you see daylight, scrape until the bottom is flat. A smooth edge is a fast edge. Using 200-grit silicone oxide sandpaper, sand away the burrs and spikes that inevitably form on ski edges.

KICK WAX

The other kind of wax is called *kick wax*. This is the wax that gives you enough grip for a strong kick. Here's where things get tricky, even mysterious. Racers hoard their waxing secrets like misers hoarding gold. But I'm going to take the mystery out of waxing. To understand the basics, you need remember only two principles:

- Hard wax is for cold, new snow, and soft wax is for warm, old snow. (When does new snow become old snow? When it's spent more than twenty-four hours on the ground.)
- The color of the wax container tells you what kind of snow it's for: cool colors like blue and green for cold days; warm colors like yellow and red for warm days; in-between colors like purple (a mixture of blue and red) for in-between days. If you're color-blind, read the label. (Jonathan Wiesel points out that when English-language instructions are at the top of the canister, and the top is the first part you peel off, my advising you to read the label may be a bit problematic. Maybe I should have said, "Memorize the label.")

If you want to keep waxing as simple as humanly possible, use an all-purpose wax—red for wet snow, blue for dry. You can get by with these two until things get really wet and warm, but they won't give you the most glide or grab for your money. For that, you need to create a coat(ing) of many colors, choosing the one most suitable for conditions on the day (or even the first half hour of the day), and even be prepared to mix and match, sometimes applying one wax over another. It's best to choose one brand of wax and stick with it. Over time, you'll get to know how to make the most of its performance characteristics.

Here's the best way to begin. Wrap a small piece of 200-grit sandpaper over your finger, and rub a series of V-shaped chevrons into the kick zone. Then put a bigger piece of sandpaper over a wood block and make a light pass over the entire kick zone, working (as you'll always work) from tip to tail. Now, heat your iron and dribble green wax over the kick zone. Green is not only a good kick wax, it's the best base wax over which you can apply all other colors. Iron it in or crayon it on; then cork it in. You need not wait to begin corking. But use a Styrofoam cork, ideally one made for ski waxing.

KLISTER

Marriage jokes are about mothers-in-law. Place jokes are about Brooklyn. Ski jokes are about klister.

Klister is sticky stuff that comes in a tube that you use when ordinary waxes won't work. Klister is to skiing as Crazy Glue is to home repair. Both stick to everything. Including fingers, hair, and your new Turtle Fur ear jock.

The trick to using klister is to avoid it whenever you can. Here's when you probably can't: When the temperature rises above freezing, and when it has risen above freezing, then cooled down again. Under these conditions, if you own waxless skis, this is the time to bring out them out. If you don't, squeeze on the klister.

Use as little as you can get away with. Use the color (yes, like waxes, klister comes in colors) that best suits the day's conditions. Follow the instructions on the label. And when your klister days are over, immediately clean it off with wax remover. Otherwise, when you bring out your skis next November, the first thing you'll see is the bases brimming with dust, twigs, dried dirt, and things too fierce to mention. The first thing you'll feel is the familiar clinging sensation as the klister magically transfers itself to your fingers, your hair, and your new Turtle Fur ear jock.

WHAT TO DO WHEN YOU'RE OUT OF WAX

You're in a cabin in the middle of nowhere. You suddenly realize that you're completely, totally out of wax. Wadda ya do?

You improvise. For glide wax, try alpine ski or snowboard wax, car wax, furniture polish, paraffin, candles, or WD-40. For kick wax, well, did you bring the skins? No? You can wrap hankies around the skis or maybe try molasses. Basically, better expect a long slog home.

NEW WAXES AND OLD STANDARDS

Waxless skis aren't the only change between skier and snow. Waxes are also changing. The leading manufacturers are constantly working to improve skier performance and, in recent years, to be environmentally friendly as well. Those leading manufacturers are based around the mountains of Europe: Swix in Norway, Rode and Solda in Italy, Toko in Switzerland, Rex and Start in Finland.

By far the biggest change in recent years is the introduction of fluorocarbon glide waxes. Here's what you need to know about fluorocarbons: They must be applied at high temperatures and give off lots of smoke and nasty gases. On a well-prepared, high-end ski on the foot of a well-trained, high-end racer, they're faster than ordinary hydrocarbon waxes. When the snow is dirty, they pick up less schmutz than ordinary waxes. And they cost up to

Winter's Diary: February 19

Weegee. I received one of the most exciting phone calls of my life. The Wyoming Department of Tourism called and asked if I would like to come on a one-week fam (short for familiarization) tour of the Jackson Hole ski region.

Would I like to come? I started packing before I hung up the receiver.

Now, along with Effin and Marsha and a couple of dogs, I'm taking my last pretrip ski through the fields of Browningron.

One of the dogs is Sophie; the other, a neighbor's old-timer named Weegee. Weegee's a fat tank of a dog, low to the ground but solid as a linebacker. Old though he is, Weegee loves the snow, and even if he didn't, he couldn't stand letting that young pup, Sophie, have all the fun of romping with us alone.

It's a brilliantly clear afternoon, and we take what's become this winter's favorite route. Starting at the back of our house, we cross the frozen pond, stride through the gate to the pasture, turn right, and ski to the end of the cornpiece fence. Then we struggle up the slope, turn left at the top of the cornpiece, and sweat our way up Hastings Hill. From the top, Browningron looks like a scenic postcard: the church at one end of town, the old schoolhouse at the other, and everything in between covered in shades of white.

We catch our breath, gather our nerve, then start down the steep back side of Hastings Hill. We're following deep snowmobile tracks and, once in them, have no way of getting out, as our edgeless cross-country skis have little in the way of turning power. When you're in the track, all you can do is hold on and enjoy the ride.

Effin's quotient of physical bravery is substantially higher than mine, and she goes first. As she swoops down the hill, both dogs follow—Sophie first, then Weegee, growling old dog curses, hard on her tail.

When all three are a safe distance ahead, I push off, settle into Effin's tracks, and lower myself into a semituck. Since there's only one way to go, I might as well go fast.

I'm halfway down the hill when I see Weegee stop, then slowly turn back. He wants to run with me. No, he's found a spot in the trail where he intends to take a nap. The spot is right at the end of the downhill run, the point at which I'll be traveling at maximum speed.

Weegee sprawls his bulk across the narrow trail.

I yell, "Weegee! Move it!"

He looks at me, either uncomprehending or faking incomprehension.

I'm going faster now. Too fast to turn. Too fast to stop. Too fast to slow down. I scream, "WEEGEE! GET OUT OF HERE!"

Weegee tentatively wags his tail. His expression is one of hurt: Why is this person yelling at me?

He shows no sign of moving.

My last thought as I hurtle toward the beast is this: If I break something and can't go to Wyoming, I'll kill that dog.

Two objects cannot occupy the same space at the same time. Weegee and I prove the truth of this law of physics when I collide with him at top speed. As he is thrown one way and I the other, his expression—a mix of puzzlement and disgust—is the last thing I see before my face is buried in snow.

Prior to getting up, I check myself for broken parts. My shoulder hurts, but I can move it. Other than that, everything more or less works. I will be able to go to Wyoming. Weegee's life is spared.

I shuffle toward home and a hot bath. Weegee trudges alongside but keeps a distance of at least 20 yards between us. From behind, Effin and Marsha are trying to sound sympathetic, but their barely suppressed laughter keeps getting in the way.

$100 an ounce. So unless you're rich and a racer, admire them from a distance, much as you would a champion racehorse or the crown jewels. By weight, they cost only slightly less.

If you're finding all this wax talk overwhelming or just plain annoying, let's go back to basics. The basic reason you took up cross-country skiing was to have fun outdoors in winter. Waxing is intended as a way to increase that fun; it is not an end unto itself. When the joys of waxing become the jobs of waxing, remember the two minimalist alternatives: Buy waxless skis; all the waxing you'll have to do is to apply a layer of glide wax halfway through the season and at winter's end. Or let a ski shop do the waxing for you. Just because you farm out unwanted work doesn't mean you're not a nice person.

Finally, a piece of advice. If you're gonna work on your own skis, treat yourself to a ski vise. After years of trying to balance my skis between a pair of mismatched bench vises, I finally sprang for a set of ski vises. What a difference! Suddenly I could wax, repair, and sharpen without having to hold my tongue in that certain position and without dark oaths echoing around my workshop. Just make sure the vise set you buy fits cross-country skis before you take it home. One more thing: If you spend a lot of time waxing and dewaxing skis, it's best to wear a protective mask.

11

Youth and Age on Skis

The opening chapter of this book talked about Jackrabbit Johannsen, who skied from age 2 to 111. Jackrabbit illustrated both of the subjects of this chapter, youth and age. This chapter is about making cross-country skiing a lifelong pleasure.

YOUTH

Let's start with the low end of the youth scale. Jackrabbit notwithstanding, if you're too young to walk without falling down every time you come to a carpet or a stone, you're too young to ski. But you're not too young to be taken

Fig. 70 *Parents with pulk*

skiing. Many skiing parents take along their young children, either in a back or front pack or in a pulk (Fig. 70), a baby carriage on runners that you pull. You can rent one at a growing number of cross-country areas. If you're a parent who runs or bikes as well as skis, you might consider investing in an Equinox Tourlite, a 19-pound baby-hauling vehicle that lets you substitute runners for wheels when the snow flies. The Equinox telephone number is (800) 942-7895.

However you carry your progeny, dress them warmly—considerably more warmly than you dress yourself. Unlike you, they're not creating body heat by moving around, and they need to be protected from the cold. If they're happy, by all means take them skiing; if they cry or whine, treat it as a sign that they've stopped enjoying the experience, and take them inside without delay. When you're bundling them up, remember the parts that get cold first—face, hands, and feet—and be sure they're wearing a hat or well-fitted hood (Fig. 71). If the air is really cold, leave the children home.

Jane Emanuelson skied every day from her Stowe, Vermont, home before she had a baby. And by Tommy's first birthday, she was skiing almost daily once again. Tommy rode in a pack on her back, from where he would enjoy the motion and then enjoy a motion-induced nap. Jane knew the transition had come when she felt Tommy's head loll to one side. Her advice to skiing parents with young children: "Dress them warmly, and check their mittens frequently—that's the item of clothing most likely to fall off. After a while, I started pinning Tommy's mittens to his snowsuit, and that worked fine."

Fig. 71

Fig. 72

When the children get older, it's time to start them on skis. They should still be dressed warmly—kids stop a lot to eat snow and do other kidlike things—and they should have equipment that fits. If their boots are too tight or ridiculously big, they are guaranteed to have a bad time . . . and make sure you get to share the experience.

BUYING EQUIPMENT FOR KIDS

Buying equipment for young kids is a lot easier than buying for adults. Why? Because you can eliminate most of the overchoice right from the git-go. For instance, you need not fret over waxed versus waxless skis. Get waxless. That will save you hassles and save your child tears of frustration when he finds he "can't make 'em go!" Don't even consider skinny racing skis for youngsters. They need a stable base beneath their wobbly legs.

As for bindings, forget about three-pin models—they're too hard to get in and out of, and they lack the stability of the NNN II and the Salomon SNS Profil systems. And don't put tykes in supersoft cheap boots or worn-out used boots. Their little ankles need a bit of bracing.

As kids get older and gear for them gets pricier, one way to save dollars is to buy combination boots that allow them to stride and skate without purchasing an extra set of expensive footwear that they'll outgrow in five weeks.

Always take advantage of swap meets to get other people's kids' skis at greatly reduced prices.

TEACHING KIDS TO SKI

Here's a spot quiz. Where should kids try skis for the first time?

A. In the woods

B. At a licensed ski area

C. In the living room

The correct answer is—the envelope, please—C, the living room. Let them get the feel of these new giant feet unencumbered by snowsuits, unchilled by winter winds, unembarrassed by staring strangers. Move the Ming Dynasty vase out of reach, and let them play around to their heart's content.

The key word is *play*. The biggest mistake parents make when teaching their children to ski is making it feel like work. You wouldn't want to ski if it reminded you of the office; kids won't ski if it reminds them of school. Or of picking up their toys.

Instead, make it fun. Rather than lecturing young skiers on the importance of balance, let them Indian wrestle on skis. Instead of talking about weight transfer, hold a contest called "Who Can Glide on One Ski the Longest?"

One of the best ways to prolong their fun is to enroll them in a kids' ski program, the most notable of which is the Bill Koch Youth Ski League. Named for America's first Olympic cross-country silver medalist, the league's mission is "to introduce young people to the lifelong sport of skiing with its recreational, social, fitness and competitive opportunities." It offers cross-country, ski jumping, and nordic combined programs for boys and girls up to thirteen years old.

There are more than one hundred clubs and nearly three thousand members across the United States, and new clubs and members are always welcome. For more information, contact the Bill Koch Youth Ski League, Box 100, Park City, UT 84060, telephone (801) 649-9090.

Finally, when planning a ski vacation with children, call the ski area in advance to confirm that they offer what you need. Depending on your youngsters' ages, that could include day care, pulks, or even narrow-gauge tracks for narrow-gauge kids.

Steve Gaskill is a former Olympic and U.S. Ski Team coach and founder of the Team Birke Ski Education Foundation, an educational resource in the Midwest aimed at raising ability level and interest in cross-country skiing and biathlon. Here's his advice on skiing with children, based on years of experience:

"Design the activities around the children, not the adults. Learn to think like your children, and be willing to ask them what they want to do and let them set the pace. Let the children play when and how they want. If they want to spend most of the time rolling down a snowbank without their skis on, why not? Let them set their goals; don't force them into accepting yours.

"Children are explorers. Let them explore as they wish. Use your energy to answer their questions and help them discover new wonders. Children will often prefer touring off the trail, through trees, under logs, and any place that adventure might lurk.

Fig. 73

"Children generally have shorter attention spans than adults. Limit the skiing time to the length that your children are happy being outside.

"Parents who show love for an activity and involve their children will teach through example. If you go out skiing and remain happy and smiling through the trip, your kids will learn that skiing is a pleasurable experience."

RESPECTING YOUR ELDERS

And now, it's time to put away childish things and start carrying the baggage of maturity. Barring global warming or some other ski disaster, the numbers of older skiers can be expected to continue their steady growth. In fact, the demographics almost guarantee it.

As we ski through the millennium, the trails are more and more likely to be filled with graying, balding, prune-slurping adults. Every year, more and more cross-country skiers will be in their forties, sixties, and even eighties, ages at which the adolescent pleasures of wretched excess—too many drinks, drugs, late nights, and fast motorcycles—have either taken their toll (as in *For Whom the Bell Tolls*) or finally worn off. Those who survived have achieved a time of life when quiet pleasures, like gliding through a spruce forest white with hoarfrost, are more appealing than blasting your brain cells with Hevy Medal and the Doomsuckers. In short, it's the perfect time to take up cross-country skiing.

Fig. 74

More than any sport I know—golf included—cross-country skiing allows you to set your own pace for speed, exertion, and even length of stretching. While cross-country skiing is rightly touted as the best aerobic conditioner, and while racers really do have quads of steel, the sport is perfectly conducive to a quiet shuffle through the woods. Skinny skiing slowly through an urban park brings different pleasures, but no less enjoyable ones, than ridge-line skiing in the Rockies or racing 55k over the hills of Gatineau Park.

For elders taking up the sport for the first time, I offer my congratulations. As the song says, You couldn't pick a better time to start in life. Cross-country skiing is one pastime in which it ain't too early and it ain't too late. I also offer the following advice:

- Start slow. Even if you're a runner or jogger, skiing uses different muscles and puts different stresses on the body. Start slow, slowly build up your speed and skills, and you'll stay fit and accident-free.
- Start flat. Don't tackle fierce uphills or dizzying downhills your first week on skis. Gradually work up (and down) to the advanced stuff from flat, then gently rolling terrain.
- Consider lessons. The best racers have coaches; why not allow yourself the same luxury? Take a lesson, and when you find an instructor you like, take another.
- Don't shortchange yourself. Stay away from low-end equipment packages. Cross-country skiing is a relatively cheap sport; it's no savings if you get gear that won't take you where you want to go.
- Give extra consideration to short and wide skis. Both are easier to learn on, and shorties require less muscle power.
- Finally, and above all, don't let age, or the idea of age, limit you. Remember Jackrabbit Johannsen, and do what you want to do.

As you age, you expect certain bodily changes—among them, weight gain and fitness loss. It feels almost inevitable yet it need not be. George M. Hall is a retired electrical engineer from Bolton, Massachusetts. In 1948, when he was thirteen and in ninth grade, he started downhill skiing. In 1962, at age twenty-seven, he tried cross-country. Today he's past sixty. Here's Hall on the changes he's seen:

"I think I paid $12 for my first cross-country skis. The boots were $28. Now I ski on Fischer Classic Cap racing skis that run about $325. The boots have gone up, too.

"I've changed, as well. When I was working, I used to ski sporadically. Sometimes I'd enter citizens' races, but I never made the time for training. But when I retired, we wanted to go north to be near the Craftsbury Outdoor Center. It's ten minutes from home, and I make pretty full use of it.

"This year my season started November 20 and didn't end until March 30. During that time I skied five to six days a week, anywhere from half an hour to two and a half hours at a time. Occasionally, when on a cross-country trek, I'd be on skis for up to six hours. Off-season, I also train: I roller-ski, run the trails at the Center, and spend time bicycling and sculling. I try to train on a regular basis. I've also become more serious about racing. I used to do low-key citizens' races. Now I ski in international competitions, including the World Masters Tournament in Italy.

"My race times have been going down, and I'm doing better in my age group than even a few years ago. Skiing is at least as enjoyable as it always was. I may need just slightly more recovery time, but not much. My weight has dropped from a little over 150 when I was forty; it's now stabilized at 145. I'm just under 5 foot 10.

"I have some advice for sixty-plus beginning skiers: Go to a touring center and start by taking a lesson. Start on tracked trails, not through untracked snow in the woods. When you buy skis, buy a nice pair. Get no-wax if you're going to be an occasional skier. A lighter ski is better than a heavier one. Avoid three-pin bindings. Get poles that come at least to your shoulders.

"You might also consider signing up for a skiing Elderhostel program. I have observed that many of the Elderhostel participants have especially enjoyed that sense of accomplishment and satisfaction that comes as they become more proficient in cross-country skiing. This is a great feeling for anyone at any age to experience."

John Brodhead directs the nordic program at Craftsbury Outdoor Center and also teaches skiing at the center's annual Elderhostel. Here are his thoughts on skiing elders:

"As years begin to accumulate, bones become more brittle, and blood gets thinner, it would seem that cross-country skiing, a sport practiced by the

Winter's Diary: March 1

Sense of Snow. As we ski through the 6 inches of powder, Effin says, "My God, it feels just like silk!" Indeed, it does—smooth, light, luxurious. I think about other snows we've skied through this year and what they felt like. There was a corduroy day, where the snow was firmly packed and fast underfoot. We had a couple of oatmeal runs through heavy, lumpy glug. And plenty of Teflon afternoons, when we effortlessly glided over an unresisting and unyielding surface.

But today is pure silk. And the luxury of skiing long bolts of it is pure pleasure.

world's most fit athletes, would be physically out of reach for older citizens. But in fact, cross-country skiing is one of the most popular activities for Elderhostelers at the Craftsbury Outdoor Center in Vermont. For seventeen years, beginning skiers age sixty and over have been learning to ski and enjoy the sport in all types of weather.

"With a few technological items, such as chemical handwarmers and electrical socks, even normally debilitating problems like poor circulation can be overcome. Activity generates its own warmth. To maintain a comfortable temperature, layered clothing is peeled off as your metabolism starts to heat up.

"Unlike the rigid boots and bindings of downhill skiing, which can snap a bone or wrench a knee during a fall, the cross-country boot-and-binding system is very supple and forgiving.

"Beginners are under control from the start. Unwanted speed is not an issue. New skiers learn on the flat where their only momentum is from self-propulsion.

"John Bland, M.D., author of *Live Long and Die Fast*, a book on quality of life while aging, is a long-time skier. At eighty he is still actively cross-country ski racing. Bland provides chapter after chapter of evidence of the benefits to health and longevity from cross-country skiing and other active outdoor pursuits. For elders, the benefits include improved bone density, joint mobility, energy, muscle strength, appetite, and mental health."

12

Caring for Yourself

OK, quiz time! Pencils ready? Which of these three sports is (are) anaerobic?

A. Downhill skiing

B. Snowboarding, dude

C. Cross-country skiing

D. A & B but not C

E. B & C but not A

And the answer is—the envelope, please—D, downhill and snowboarding. Cross-country is the only aerobic sport of the three. Aerobic means sustained cardiovascular activity as opposed to a lot of starts and stops. It means that once you start moving, you keep on moving. That's cross-country, all right.

And the best kind of body conditioning you can do to get ready for the season is aerobic. Move and keep moving. Take vigorous walks. Go for long, meditative swims. Bicycle to the next town or neighborhood. Climb the stairs instead of taking the elevator. Get off the bus three stops early and walk briskly the rest of the way to work. Sell your ride-on mower and snow blower. Cut up firewood the old-fashioned way.

Note that I don't say the E word, "e-x-e-r-c-i-s-e." That's for strong-willed people, people with a high tolerance for boredom, people who floss before and after meals of lettuce and kale. People different from, say, us.

Why is exercise so excruciatingly dull? Because exercise is physical activity to promote fitness. And there's nothing as boring as doing one thing for the sake of something else, especially something else as worthy, healthy, and good for you as fitness promotion.

I hate exercise. I have to do some to keep my back from assuming the permanent shape of a pretzel, but even with that incentive, it's hard to maintain. Yet I manage to stay reasonably fit the whole year through. Here's how.

Fig. 75 *Exercise—Jules Older style*

When I'm in a hotel or university, I walk the stairs—two at a time unless I'm carrying luggage—rather than take the elevator. I move snow with a Jules-propelled scoop, about 100 inches of it every winter. I have a plain, non-self-propelled power mower, and if I'm not running behind it, I'm walking fast. I'm also walking fast on our near-daily shake-out-the-cobwebs trek up the hill in front of our home. We go two or three miles, half steep uphill and half down. On days we don't walk, we take out the mountain bikes for an hour or so. Effin and I cut firewood with an old two-person (formerly two-man) saw. And whenever we get the chance, we indulge in the best aerobic exercise of all, dancing.

Though it's every bit as physical, dancing is the complete opposite of exercise. In the history of the world, no one was ever bored when dancing with a sensuous partner. Dancing is vigorous, exciting, romantic, sexually arousing, and still legal in most states. The difference between dancing and wrestling is that some holds are barred in wrestling.

For physical fitness without exercise, you might also try wrestling. But only if you can't dance.

Cycling is a much better alternative. The beauty of cycling is that, like skiing, it builds your leg muscles without jamming your bones into the ground every time you take a step. The other beauty of cycling is that it gets you from point A to point B faster than any other form of self-propelled mobility. And as you know, I am fond of anything that gets you where you want to go.

But note that cycling must not be confused with Exercycling. Pedaling a bike going nowhere is—well, there's no other word for it—it's exercise.

Still, for those who live in miserable climates and those who are chained to the indoors, exercise is better than nothing. Anything that increases your fitness will add to your skiing enjoyment, improve your prowess, and probably lessen your chance of injury. What you want is exercise that will mimic skiing—full-body muscle workout, a lot of stretching, and a healthy dose of sustained aerobic activity, formerly called stamina.

Here's some of what's available:

- *NordicTrack.* The mother of all ski exercisers, NordicTrack provides a skilike experience involving both legs and arms. It's without a doubt the most highly advertised workout machine in North America. (800) 445-2231.
- *Sky Trek.* My own favorite. Though not as well known, I find it gives a better workout and takes you on a wilder ride than NordicTrack. It also better mimics cross-country skiing's long, diagonal stride. And it comes with optional hydraulics to intensify the workout. It's sold by FitnessQuest, (800) 321-9236.
- *Pro Fitter.* Unlike NordicTrack or Sky Trek, Pro Fitter works both feet at the same time, and primarily side to side rather than fore and aft. That makes it better for downhill and snowboard prep than for cross-country skiing, but I like it for everything. It builds balance as well as strength and stamina, and it's one of the few exercisers with a learning curve. That makes it harder to get bored on a Pro Fitter than on most other gadgets. It's made by Fitter International, (800) FITTER-1.
- *Exerstrider.* One of my favorite gadgets, the Exerstrider costs only about $60 and is used outside more than in. It's little more than a pair of ski poles with modified hand grips and rubber cups instead of bas-

kets and points at the bottom. Exerstrider allows you to build upper-body exercise into walks and jogs without the risk of injury associated with hand weights. I love anything that lets you do two things at the same time. Can you make your own faux Exerstriders by cutting the points and baskets off an old pair of poles and adding rubber cups? Sure. But you can get the premade (and probably better-made) item for less than the cost of your time, and it comes with an instructional video. (800) 554-0989.

- *Vew-Do.* Now this is wild. Vew-Do is a board and a tapered wooden cylinder, and there are an infinite number of tricks you can do when you put board on cylinder, feet on board, and start learning to balance. If you remember the old Bongo Board, this is the same thing on ganja. Much more fun than exercise. Vew-Do costs around $120 and is made by Balance Designs (802) 362-7098.
- *Exercycle.* OK, OK. The stationary bicycle is a good way to keep your legs from turning to Jell-O after the Indian summer and before the snow flies. But be sure to bring a book or video, or you risk death by terminal boredom.
- *Roller skis.* Many American racing coaches consider off-season roller skiing essential to maintaining winter fitness and balance. Coach Lee Borowski even says, "If a skier wishes to excel . . . the only solution is roller skiing." That's quite a tribute to a device most Americans have never heard of, much less seen. The roller ski is halfway between a roller skate and an old-fashioned scooter, a pair of in-line wheels set at either end of a bar fitted with a ski binding. They're fast, they require lots of energy, and they're a fair mimic for the skills of skiing.

  They're also kind of dangerous, especially on downhills, since their brakes are usually less efficient than those of in-line skates, and many have no brakes at all. In *Don't Look Back*, former Dartmouth coach John Morton describes watching his team racing on roller skis and suddenly realizing that they were headed for a long, curving downhill onto a covered bridge. He ran to his car, raced ahead of them, and grabbed each one by the seat of the pants as they hit the top of the hill, slowing them down by dragging his feet until they were halfway down the hill.

  Since I'm a certified coward and don't have a coach waiting for me at the top of the hill, I avoid roller skis.
- *In-line skates.* Less risky and more popular than roller skis, in-line skates (Rollerblades, Bauer, Oxygen, and the like) also combine an aerobic workout, leg strengthening, balance building, and fun. They, too, are kind of dangerous, especially in traffic and most especially if

you're not wearing helmet, knee and elbow pads, and gloves. The major difference between falling on asphalt and falling on snow is that on snow, you slide; on asphalt, you grind. Wear protective gear.

- *Nordixc.* Safer and cheaper than roller skis, more stable and energy burning than in-line skates, Nordixc is a three-wheeled device with built-in brakes that gives a fair imitation of cross-country skiing in the muscles it uses. It costs $370 and is made by V2 Jenex. (603) 672-2600.
- *Skiing.* Oh, and do not neglect skiing as a way of getting in shape for skiing. You use exactly the same muscles and have precisely the same amount of fun. And it's a proven fact, the more you ski, the more prepared you'll be for skiing.

  To add to the benefits of this activity, you might consider some warm-ups before the first run of the day, followed by a few decent stretches. Nothing painful or boring, of course. Not exercise. Just a bit of stomping around in the snow, swinging your arms in circles. Then plant your poles, slide one leg forward and the other back, and hold it for a minute. Reverse for another minute, and you're ready to face the day.

HEALTH BENEFITS OF CROSS-COUNTRY SKIING

According to sports physician and skier Dr. Peter Dorson, cross-country skiing is the best cardiovascular winter exercise available. It should be. How many other activities combine low impact and high fat burning, low injury and high metabolism, low weight and high endurance, and use all the body's major muscle groups?

A word about that phrase "low weight." In addition to using all the major muscle groups, cross-country skiing uses them in winter, and according to Dr. Jim Stray-Gundersen, the director of sports medicine for the U.S. Cross-Country Ski Team, "The cold weather associated with cross-country skiing increases the caloric expenditure, since the body also uses more calories in an effort to maintain body heat." By his estimates, the average male recreational cross-country skier burns about 600 calories an hour, and the average female burns 400 to 500. Stray-Gundersen also believes that cross-country skiing can reduce cholesterol levels.

All these benefits are great, yet the best benefits of cross-country skiing are even greater. No one has described this better than Fridtjof Nansen, the great Norwegian explorer who traversed Greenland on cross-country skis more than a century ago. He wrote in 1890: "Nothing hardens the muscles and makes the body so strong and elastic. Nothing gives better presence of mind and nimbleness; nothing steels the will power and freshens the mind as cross-country skiing. This is something that develops not only the body but also the soul—it has a far deeper meaning for people than many are aware of."

Mark Lichtenstein, who practices family medicine and cross-country skis in Hardwick, Vermont, prescribes cross-country skiing to many of his patients.

"For exercise, cross-country skiing is one important option here in Vermont's Northeast Kingdom. It's inexpensive, available as an individual or group activity, and adaptable, even to people with multiple disabilities. What's more, cross-country skiing can be easily customized to make it suitable for all abilities and levels of fitness.

"Cross-country skiing exercises flexor and extensor leg muscles without undue stress on the knees and hips. It is remarkably kind to the elderly and the arthritic. It is safe, when practiced with even a minimum of intelligence with regard to risk taking. Compare skiing with jogging: Skiing is much easier on the knees and hips, gives good upper-body exercise, and allows for more adaptation to personal fitness levels.

"An important benefit (outside of the aerobic workout effect on your heart, lungs, circulation, immune function, and cholesterol levels) is the meditative quality of the rhythmic exercise. This is aerobic meditation, and like many martial arts, it is a wonderful form of relaxation. Such a combination of mental, psychological, emotional, and spiritual exercise is important—it addresses mind and body health needs simultaneously."

CROSS-COUNTRY AND ALPINE

Cross-country skiing can be a great complement to alpine skiing. Suzanne Roy and Lucie Garneau work at Mont-Sainte-Anne, Quebec, one of North America's leading alpine and cross-country resorts. Here's what they have to say on the relationship between these cousin sports.

"Alpine skiers sometimes view cross-country skiing as opposite to alpine, when they should see it as complementary. It's a great cardiovascular training sport, and it exercises the upper body as much as the lower.

"Whereas alpine skiing is mostly muscular, cross-country skiing is a long-duration sport that will help improve your general physical condition. No matter how in shape or out of shape you are, cross-country is accessible as a low-, medium-, or high-intensity activity, depending on your speed, choice of trail, and technique. Furthermore, unlike what alpine skiing can do to your knees, for example, the fluidity of cross-country motions is gentle to your body, avoiding premature wear on joints.

"Being an alpine skier, you already have good balance and a knowledge of weight transfer, which gives you a head start. You now have to learn to control your skis, even with the loose heels that may feel awkward at first. Taking a one- or two-hour lesson is a good way to start. You should begin with short distances, even if you feel very comfortable on the cross-country trails. Otherwise, you might painfully find out that the muscles and joints at work in cross-country are not the same as in alpine.

"Try cross-country skiing and discover new scenery and new ways to enjoy winter in the snow!"

STAYING WARM

One painless way to stay warm is to eat a big breakfast. Because digestion creates body heat, a well-fed skier is more likely to be a warm skier. Combine fruit for instant warmth with grains and spuds for long-lasting heat and, of course, lots of eggs and sausage for extra cholesterol.

Make microadjustments in your clothing during the day. Zip up on the downhills; drop a layer before climbing. If it's not too cold, take off your gloves and hat now and then to give the moisture a chance to evaporate.

If you've bought wicking underwear and are still wet, switch from an all-cotton turtleneck to a natural-synthetic blend. Polyester wicks better than cotton, and the farther from your body the sweat is transported, the faster it evaporates.

Finally, treat the windchill factor with respect, but don't let it frighten you. The factor measures the combined effect of wind and temperature on exposed flesh. As veteran ski patroller and ski journalist Dave Irons says, "Aside from a couple of streakers and a few bikinis and shorts at Tuckerman Ravine in May, I haven't seen much exposed flesh on skiers." According to Irons, the time for concern is when the actual temperature sinks down into the low single numbers or below. But with continuing improvements in underwear, footwear, and handwear, and with a dollop of common sense about the cold, skiers can enjoy themselves in almost any weather.

TRAIL FOOD

The traditional trailside snack carries the poetic name "gorp." Gorp is typically a mix of raisins and peanuts, carried in a sack and dragged out during rest stops. But nuts are hard to digest, particularly at times of physical stress, like a day of bushwhacking or a 15k race. Gorp can be redesigned to fit your energy needs and taste buds. This is how Effin describes gorp in her kid's book, *The Super-Cool Summer Camp Kit*:

"Here's what you need: chocolate bar, nuts, raisins. Here's how you make it: Chop the chocolate and nuts into little pieces. Mix them with raisins. Put the mixture in a plastic bag. Nibble. P.S. You can be creative when you're making gorp by adding granola, Cheerios, M&Ms, chocolate chips, coconut, dried fruit—whatever you fancy." Effin obviously doesn't worry unduly about these hard-to-digest nuts. Today, along with just about everything else,

Winter's Diary: March 9

Races! Most of our ski jaunts end with a race. The course is a longish downhill, ending in a very long run-out. Since I'm bigger, my weight is an advantage. But Effin's tuck is tighter, and somehow, though I waxed both our skis, hers run faster. Other handicaps and excuses: The dogs got in my way. You chose a faster line. I said we could only pole three times. The gods hate me. And, what's the big deal? I don't ski for speed.

gorp has been prepackaged. An ever-growing number of competing companies also produce high-energy bars, available at outdoors shops, sports stores, and supermarkets. Buy them to suit your taste. Here's how my taste buds respond to some of the commercial products.

- *PowerBar.* The best known of the energy bars, PowerBar reminds me of a combination of week-old saltwater taffy and cardboard. I'm sure the energy required to chew it outpulls the energy gain it offers.
- *Gu.* OK, it could use a new name. But despite its unappealing moniker and the fact that you squeeze it out of a tube Apollo 13–style, Gu isn't half bad. Vanilla bean tastes nothing like vanilla; caramel bean would be more like it, but as long as you can find a water chaser, it tastes pretty good and is superconvenient to carry.
- *Nutri Power Enigize.* Oats, apple juice, dates, raisins, pineapple, papaya, honey, vanilla, and bee pollen sounds terribly healthy, but it results in a bar with the flavor of dried fruit and the texture of chewy nougat. Not bad. And since it was created by Ramy Amier, a former soccer player and Olympic weight lifter, it's designed to be good for athletes who need strength and endurance.
- *Vel.* My fave by far. Vel is made in Canada and contains sesame and sunflower seeds, four kinds of nuts, citrus peel, and several fruits. At room temp, it's so soft you have to tooth it out of the plastic, but if you like sesame, its taste is way better than health food should be.

Jean Arthur did her own taste test on energy bars and gels for the March 1997 *Back Country* magazine. Here, in brief, is what she and her nordic tasters found:

- *Torque Bar.* The testers' hands-down favorite. Its one downfall is its relatively high moisture content—it freezes solid at about 0 degrees Fahrenheit (as do all the other bars tested here).

- *Okanagan Sport.* A 100 percent natural Canadian bar with more flavor (some found it had too much flavor) than all others.
- *Extreme Survival.* The honey nut and peanut butter–chocolate chip bars are considerably drier than Okanagan or Torque, and the testers were skeptical of the first ingredient, rice syrup.
- *Blast.* Gel that comes in grape, coffee, sourberry, and cherry cola. Blast is made of primarily water with a carbohydrate blend of rice syrup and maltodextrin.
- *PowerGel.* A new puddinglike product in four flavors. PowerGel needs an accompanying 8 to 20 ounces of water. You can eat it fast and digest it quickly, but the package leaves a sticky mess in your pocket.
- *Hammer Gel.* Billed as a "rapid energy athletic fuel," Hammer Gel vanilla was described by one tester as "downright nasty with a hideous after taste." The chocolate fared somewhat better.

13

Caring for the Environment

Some stuff is so obvious it shouldn't need saying. And if there weren't so much evidence that it does need saying, I wouldn't say it. Here goes:

- Don't litter the countryside.
- Don't start a forest fire.
- Don't leave anything behind but ski tracks.

Good. Now let's get to the less obvious. Starting with closing gates. Throughout North America, many farmers will happily let hikers and skiers make their way through their property. Whenever possible, it's a courtesy to ask, but there's something even more important: *Close the gate behind you.*

Fig. 76 *Closing the gate*

Even if the gate holds together a rickety wire fence in the middle of the woods, it's there for a purpose. Most likely, the purpose is to keep livestock in or out of an area. It's fine to unhitch the gate long enough to let you and your party through (though, if the fence wires are strung between porcelain knobs, you'd best touch only the rubber handle when you unhitch it). But once you're through, you've got to close the gate behind you. Nothing is worse for a farmer's temper than to find that the Holsteins have gotten out through the gate you left open, and nothing is more likely to shut off the property to the next party of skiers. Whatever else you do, close the gate behind you.

In *The New Cross-Country Ski Book*, former Olympic coach John Caldwell offers this sage advice on getting along with property owners: "You often hear pleas for respecting the landowners . . . but I think it's great if you can go that extra step and make the landowners respect you as a skier. Search them out to thank them. You might come across a situation where you help them out with a mere 5 or 10 minutes' work shoveling snow, or . . . stacking some wood. I can guarantee you the landowners will never forget experiences like this. And neither will you."

Another no-no is fouling streams. While that might seem as obvious as "don't litter," most city dwellers, unfamiliar with any hydro system other than running water, aren't sure how to avoid fouling streams. Here are four rules to live by:

- Dispose of food waste well away from any standing water. Bury it in a shallow trench or scatter it over the forest floor, or better still, pack waste out just as you packed the food in.
- Do your dishwashing, hair washing, and toothbrushing well away from surface water, and if possible, use biodegradable soap.
- If outhouses are provided, use them. If not, imitate your cat. Dig a shallow hole at least 100 feet from water, mix the waste with the soil (assuming the soil isn't frozen solid), and cover it with a pile of leaves and twigs. If the snow is too high to reach soil, dig your snow pit as deep as you can, and cover the waste with snow.
- Keep the dog out of the water, and clean up any mess Rover leaves on the trail.

Finally, let us discuss a sensitive topic: cross-country skiers and snowmobilers. Let's look at them—what the heck, let's caricature them.

Cross-country skiers have open faces, chapped lips, and fabulous calf muscles. They like skiing because it gives them a chance to exercise those muscles without too much competitiveness and without Harming The Environment. They secretly believe that if they ski enough, they'll live forever.

Winter's Diary: March 15

Sense of Smell. When I skied through the pine grove, I distinctly smelled balsam. Spring.

Beneath their visors, snowmobilers have sparkling eyes, pale complexions, and trembling fingers, the result of a 50-mile ride they've just completed. They like racing across snowy fields with friends and family. They also like being in charge of a powerful machine that takes them wherever they command it.

Unlike, say, mountain bikers and pedestrians, skiers and snowmobilers live in relative harmony. They're neighbors with a similar love of cold-weather outdoor recreation. But now let's leave skis and snowmobiles for a moment. Let's talk about biological relationships.

Remember in high school biology, when you learned about symbiosis? Symbiosis, you may recall, is a mutually advantageous relationship between two living organisms. A good example is the yucca plant of the American Southwest. One species of yucca depends on a small insect, the Pronuba moth, for pollination. The moth depends on the yucca to complete its life cycle. Neither species could survive without the other. That's symbiosis.

It's nice to think of skiers and snowmobilers as symbiotic. They share the same outdoors at the same season and often use the same trails for their recreation.

It's nice to think of them as symbiotic, but they're not.

In high school biology, you learned of another relationship in nature. This one's called parasitism. Parasitism is where one species lives off another, giving little or nothing back. The flea is a parasite to the dog. The pinworm is a parasite to the human. And friends, the cross-country skier is a parasite to the snowmobiler.

Yes, there it is. Skiers give nothing back to snowmobilers; rather, they live off the fruits of their labor. Though both groups share the same outdoors and the same season and the same trails, it is snowmobilers who make and maintain the trails. Skiers just use them.

(There's another winter relationship that is worse than parasitism. All-terrain vehicle drivers not only use the snowmobile trails, they often damage them with their big, treaded tires. This is known as an aggressor relationship. There's plenty of that in nature, too.)

It's true that most snowmobilers don't mind sharing their trails with skiers. And it's true that breaking trails is much easier with a snow machine than with a narrow pair of skis. But it's also true that mutually beneficial relationships are more satisfying than one-sided relationships. Symbiosis makes everybody happy.

Is there a way to turn this parasitism to symbiosis? The easiest way is for skiers who use snowmobile trails to join a local snowmobile club and roll up their sleeves. Their dues and their help on workdays will go a long way toward evening the balance. There's nothing like working together to cement a relationship.

Once they've joined the club and helped with the trail work, there is something else skiers can do, something that will contribute to both groups' mutual safety: They can stay off the trails on weekends and holidays. Although cross-country skiing is thought of as a silent sport, the *whoosh* of skis on snow is just loud enough to mask the sound of an approaching snowmobile. Snowmobiles move with remarkable speed along those trails, and the skier who is *whoosh-whooshing* along in a dreamy state stands a real chance of getting retreaded. (See chapter 7 for a discussion of snowmobiles and skiing safety.)

14

Getting Ready for Snow

Winter is coming. Snow will fall. You read it here first.

For cross-country skiers, the coming of winter snows is reason for celebration. But celebrations are best when you're prepared to enjoy them. Don't think of skiing as a surprise party but as an affair you want to dress up for.

Dressing up for skiing starts with equipment: boots, bindings, skis, and skiwear. Here's how to get them ready for their winter debut.

BOOTS

Start with ski boots, and start by cleaning them with a sponge and mild soap. If you stored your boots in the cellar, check carefully for mold, and give those spots an extra cleaning. Next year, store them in a closet, not in the heat of the attic or the dampness of the basement.

If your boots are made of leather, air-dry them without excess heat; then clean them with saddle soap. Next, apply a moistureproofing compound. Ah, but which one? For years, mink oil was the waterproofer of choice. Then Sno-Seal. Then Biwell. They all worked; they all still do. But today's favorite waterproofer is a high-tech compound called Nikwax. You apply it when the leather or fabric (it works on both) is wet, and its water-repellent polymers bond to the fibers, leaving the space between them unclogged and breathable. Nikwax makes other waterproofers for down garments, sleeping bags, and even ropes and is available at most ski and outdoor shops.

Then check the foot beds. If they look flat, it's time to throw them away. Do the same with frayed laces. Don't wait to discover faulty equipment 5 miles from nowhere in the middle of a blizzard.

If you have shoe trees, use them (and remember to use them next spring as well); if not, stuff old newspapers in your boots and stick them in that great storage cliché, a cool, dry place.

BINDINGS

Last spring, you made sure your bindings were free from road salt before putting them away. You did that, didn't you? Just in case you didn't, do it now. Use a household cleaner, a soft rag, and a fair amount of elbow grease. Salt corrodes metal parts; that's why bindings and skis should be on a permanent salt-free diet.

Of course, prevention is the best medicine, and the best prevention is keeping your bindings covered when they're on the road—especially the salty roads of snow country. If you've got a station wagon to throw them in, that's ideal, but if not, consider buying a ski bag or carrier for the roof rack. Oh, and clean the salt off the roof rack, too.

SKIS

Like boots and bindings, skis should be stored in a cool, dry place, such as a first-floor closet. Prolonged exposure to moisture shortens their lives. The best way to store skis, summer and winter, is to hang them rather than lean them against the wall. Hang the skis, tips up, between two dowels, with another two near the tails. Or put them in a vertical rack where they can drain free of left-on snow. Effin made one for our skis in about ten minutes, using two strips of scrap lumber and a few nails. But once your skis are in the racks, don't strap the bottoms together. Although it's not the issue it was in the days of wooden skis, flattening skis works against their built-in camber.

For those who do their own tuning, here's another tip: When you give your boards a postseason wax in the spring, wax thickly, ironing it over the edges and even the sidewalls. Store your skis that way, and don't scrape off the excess wax until just before your first run. Not only will your steel edges (if you have 'em) gain maximum rust protection, but the hot wax gets absorbed into the base and makes the skis faster and more immune to impact.

SHOP WORK

If you don't do your own tuning, have your skis shop tuned now rather than waiting until the first snow. When the snow flies, shops suddenly find themselves overflowing with deeply gouged, dull-edged skis, all marked "Rush!" They're so rushed you could get a rush job . . . or even miss the first day of skiing.

Don't be afraid to ask questions about the shop. How satisfied are their customers? How experienced are their tuners? How up-to-date is their equipment? And be sure they have experience with nordic skis, not just alpines. Remember—they're different sports with different equipment and require different maintenance skills.

If you're going to prepare your skis at home, here's what you should know: If your skis are plastic or fiberglass, they aren't fussy about preseason preparation; a soapy cloth should do fine.

Wooden skis are more finicky. If the top of the ski is oiled, give it a healthy dose of linseed oil. If it's lacquered and the lacquer is cracked, sand and relacquer. (Actually, polyurethane is better than true lacquer. Ask your hardware store for advice as to brand and type.) Then, turn the skis over and pine-tar the bottoms. Pine-tarring involves burning pitch into the wood. Spread it on with a brush—an old brush—then burn it in with a butane or propane torch. The gunk should be hot enough to bubble but not to smoke. When the skis dry, put a 2-by-4 block between them to keep their camber, and hang them up until snow covers the trails.

CLOTHING

"Unless you want your new parka to fade, store it in a blue bag, not a clear one," says John Smith, former customer relations manager of Bogner Skiwear. "And when you have it cleaned, have it Scotchgarded at the same time. It will be more water repellent, especially when you're eating lunch on an ice-covered log with wet snow falling on your shoulders."

Should you wash or dry clean ski outerwear? Many brands of skiwear carry labels that say to dry clean only, on the theory that they're safer when they're cleaned by professionals. If you decide to do them at home instead, watch out for a washing machine that twists garments, watch out for residues of bleach or dyes left in the machine, and watch out for your own carelessness.

If you do wash your duds, follow the instructions on the label. Then dry them at low heat. If you have a parka (or sleeping bag) filled with down or other high-loft insulations, throw a tennis shoe (preferably a clean tennis shoe) into the dryer. The shoe fluffs up the feathers and fillings.

While you're washing, you can renew the fabric's water repellence by emptying a bottle of Du Pont Sport Water Repeller (about $10; call 800-248-0425) into the washing machine along with your ski duds. That's all there is to it.

Use as big a hanger as you can when storing ski jackets. Nylon bends, and if the hanger isn't long enough, your expensive jacket will develop an unsightly pimple in the middle of each shoulder. Zip the zipper; then put the whole lot in a blue plastic bag. Jackets with high-loft insulation—ones that look fat even when they're on thin people—should be stored in a dry place, because that fat insulation absorbs humidity.

To keep from developing unsightly fat yourself, don't put your body in storage, not even in a cool, dry place. Better to flex that bod, strengthen it, enjoy it. Then, when snow finally falls, you'll enjoy it even more.

Winter's Diary: March 16

Vive la Différence. After two days of downhill skiing with a bunch of ski writers, the next morning we all strap on cross-country skis. *Vive la différence!* Among my colleagues, I'm low-average as a downhiller. When we race, which we do every time we meet, I usually come in two-thirds the way down the pack.

But today, on cross-country skis, I'm The Man. My buddies can't figure out how to balance on these skinny boards. They're having trouble getting a grip on the snow. And when they try to skate, their right ski tangles with their left, leaving them prone—and I don't mean prone to argue.

All this comes as a surprise to me. Because I ski most days, the balance, the grip, the angled stride all seem natural and very, very easy. It looks like practice does make—well, not perfect, but compared with my pals floundering in the snowdrifts, purty durned good.

CARING FOR THE CAR

Besides your skis, clothes, and bod, there is one other thing to take care of before snow falls—the vehicle that's going to get you where you want to go. This is not an afterthought; your car not only stands between getting there and sitting in front of a closed gas station in a howling gale, but can also stand between life and death.

Start your winter prep where the rubber meets the road. Though all-season treads are better than they used to be, if you drive in snow country—unless you have four-wheel or all-wheel drive—I strongly advise you to get snow tires. Along with most of my Vermont neighbors, I use them on all four wheels. Under most conditions, they give better grip and surer stopping power.

Next, make sure your engine oil is winter-grade and that your windshield washer is filled with washer fluid, which contains antifreeze, rather than water, which doesn't. Squirt lubricating oil or WD-40 in the door locks. Change those old wiper blades. And go to your store's automotive department and get yourself a bottle of Rain-X.

Driving home from Stowe one summer night, I ran into a sudden rain squall. But for the first two minutes, I didn't know it was raining, much less pouring. The raindrops bounced off the windshield so fast I didn't see them. Throughout the ten-minute downpour, I never turned on my wipers.

How come? Earlier that day I'd applied Rain-X to the windshield. Rain-X is "an ultra-thin, absolutely invisible polymer coating that fills the microscopic pores of glass and transparent plastics with inert, hydrophobic molecules that are chemically and physically bonded to the surface like an invisible shield.'"

And I didn't even know glass had pores. What I know now is that this stuff works. It works on rain, snow, frost, ice, and even bugs—they all bounce off the glass. And the manufacturer swears that it adds amazing glide to cross-country and downhill skis.

But a word of caution—Rain-X works only if you follow the (simple) directions. The first time I tried it, I didn't bother reading the label, and Rain-X didn't bother sealing my windshield's pores.

15

When Things Go Wrong

All right, Jules, we know you've been dying to tell us your Newfoundland story. Let's have it now.

Actually, I was thinking it might be instructive—how quickly conditions change in the mountains and the preparations you can make to –

Skip the sermon and just get on with the story

Right. Here's the story . . .

The phone woke us. Dan Chaisson's laconic Newfoundland voice barely concealed his excitement: "Be ready at nine—we've got a helicopter waiting at ten to fly us in."

We were ready, all right. After four days of waiting for a break in the weather, we were more than ready.

We needed calm winds for a day of backcountry skiing on the Lewis Hills, Newfoundland's highest peaks, and despite the midnight forecast of storms, at last we had it.

Dan was just as ready. He picked us up early from our hotel in downtown Corner Brook, then picked up Ian Hutchinson from his physiotherapy office. Through a rare morning of April sunshine, the four of us drove to Universal Helicopters, where Ian changed in the hangar from shirt and tie to ski gear. As the Long Ranger chopper carried us over snow-covered forests and ice-covered bay, I felt the tingling pleasure that comes with undeserved good fortune.

That was then.

This is 4:30 in the afternoon, and the four of us—guides Ian and Dan, photographer Effin, and I—are skiing across the broad, undulating summit of the Lewis Hills.

All day the snow has been tricky—strips of windblown powder alternating with rough ice. Our skis sound like Danny's Big Wheel in *The Shining* —

whoosh, silence, *whoosh*, silence, *whoosh*. Except for the snow, the summit is naked. We've seen not a single tree or shrub—only the snow and the rough, red rocks that push through the snowscape like strawberries poking out of a cheesecake, strangely colored mushrooms through a forest floor.

Lewis Hills may be the highest peaks in Newfoundland, but by most standards they're not very high, and they're not true peaks but dozens of minisummits ranging from 2,000 to 2,672 feet above sea level. To the north, the summits overlook the sea—we gaze down through deep-cut canyons on the ice-bound Gulf of St. Lawrence—and they're surrounded on all other sides by dense forest. Because of its northern latitude, the entire top is well above treeline. It's also exposed, windy, and remote. We were helicoptered in because that's the only way to get there in a single day, and we plan to ride out on snow machines.

Fig. 77 *Lewis Hills*

Since we first put on skis at 11 A.M., the sun's been shining, the temperature's squatted just below 30, and the breeze has been brisk but tolerable. It's been a fine day for backcountry skiing and photography.

Just after 4:30, Dan points out a herd of caribou hovering on the horizon, and we all notice the dark-bottomed cumulus cloud hovering above them. Within minutes, both caribou and horizon have disappeared, and the cloud, darker still, is closing in fast. Very fast.

Our plan has been to meet George Pike sometime between 4 and 5 at the tiny Hinds Pond hut, anchored to frozen ground somewhere on these endlessly rolling summits. From there, he's going to ferry us on snow vehicles off the mountain and down 30 miles of snow-covered logging road to his lodge. Dan carries a walkie-talkie, and he's been trying to raise George on it all afternoon. Every hour on the quarter hour he pulls out the squawk box and intones, "George Pike, George Pike. Do you read?"

He's never gotten through.

Both Dan and Ian have been to the Hinds Pond hut before, and both are carrying maps and compasses. Somehow, Ian's compass broke during lunch; still, one is all we need to guide us. But just as they're about to take their final reading, the dark cloud storms over us, obscuring all landmarks and everything else that's more than a ski length away.

I've skied in whiteouts; this is more of a charcoal-grayout. The air has a dark, damp bleakness that chills my soul more than my body. I shiver against cold . . . and the first sensation of fear.

And then I realize something's wrong. For the first time all day, Dan and Ian are whispering. Their hushed conference is animated by map pointing and compass checking. Effin and I glance silently at each other.

As I step from one ski to the other for warmth, I eavesdrop on the guides. Ian thinks the hut is to the left; Dan thinks it's to the right. After more whispering and pointing, they choose left.

We ski down out of the cloud toward the treeline until we find ourselves on a ridge overlooking a steep, icy gulch. It looks ugly, and after six hours on skis, we're beginning to feel ugly and more than a little fearful. We know it, but we don't show it. The guides have enough to handle without our apprehension.

The gulch certainly isn't skiable, and I'm not entirely sure it's walkable. Suddenly Dan's walkie-talkie squawks. "Dan, Dan. Come in, Dan. This is George. Do you read?"

All four of us shout, "We read! We read!" It sounds like graduation day at the slow-learners' class.

We breathe a collective sigh of relief. Help is near—or at least within walkie-talkie range. But our relief is premature.

We now have to figure out how we're going to get to George, or he to us. We don't know precisely where we are, and we can't tell where he is. So now we face a second decision—turn left and head into the depths of the gulch that separates us from George, wherever he is, or turn right, climb a sharply inclined hill, and circle around the other way. The guides confer and choose the hill.

We discover that the hill was a bad choice when Ian, who is leading the procession, twice loses his foothold and falls while climbing its ice-encrusted side. Both times he hits the frozen surface with a stomach-churning thud. What's worse, Ian is clad in heavy-soled telemark boots, and the rest of us are wearing lighter gear; if he can't make it, we don't stand a chance.

With rapidly ebbing spirits, we turn around, climb back down, and trudge up to the ridge where we'd been standing a half hour before. I always find it depressing to backtrack, especially on an icy and quickly darkening mountain. Had we been voting, I would have cast one ballot for dropping down into the slick and treacherous gulch toward the woods. At least it was down.

By now the air is dark, cold—about minus 15 with the windchill—and thick with cloud. We're losing heat and using up energy, and we're right back where we started. Ian says firmly, "Wait here! I'm gonna look again for that hut." He skis off into the cloud. Dan says, "Wait here! I'm gonna climb that hill and try to find another way out."

Effin and I wait. We feel very much alone in a cold, dark, and entirely unfamiliar place. We do a silent dance, trying to keep warm. She asks, "Can we survive a night on the mountain?"

I answer, "Sure, no trouble." But I'm not as sure as I try to sound, and she can hear the false heartiness in my voice.

Dan once again tries to scale the icy hill. From where he clings to the steep side, he can talk to George but can't see him. Dan shouts a relayed message to Effin and me: "Can you see lights?"

"No . . . Yes!"

"One or two?"

"One . . . no, two!"

George has moved his snow machines to a high point of land about a mile away, well below the treeline. He's flashing us signals from his Argo—an open, tracked, twin-headlighted vehicle—to make sure it's his lights we see. Dan scurries back down the hill just as Ian skis out of the cloud shouting, "Found it—I found the hut! Follow me!"

We tell George where we're headed, then ski toward the hut. From the other side of the mountain, George speeds off to meet us.

But it's not over yet.

First we trudge back uphill, carrying our skis and using the poles to keep from slipping on the icy surface. When we reach the frozen pond, we put on the skis and slog across the ice toward a black flyspeck Ian assures us is the Hinds Pond hut. The cloud has lifted, but night has fallen; we ski in darkness. And now the wind is up, whipping a river of blowing snow over our skis and into our eyes. It takes us almost an hour to reach the tiny hut.

Winter's Diary: March 21

Psychological Spring. We are experiencing spring conditions, which is to say, we never know what the next day or the next kick is going to bring. Fields of slush, patches of ice, crust that clatters like a rattlesnake's tail—we've got it all. The trickiest is the solid-looking snow that drops you a foot as soon as you put weight on it.

By the end of an afternoon's outing, we feel more like the three bears than the three skiers. Despite the fact that we all have the same klister on our skis, Marsha's are too fast, Effin's are too sticky, and mine are just right. After struggling through rapidly changing conditions on her newly unresponsive skis while wearing first too few clothes, then too many, Effin describes spring as menopausal winter: "Cold flashes, hot flashes—you never know what to expect next."

When we manage to wrench open the door against the storm, we step into a room the size of a largish closet. If anything, it's colder than outside. We quickly discover that while the hut has four cramped and unblanketed bunk beds, there's not a candle, not a match, and not a stick of kindling in the wretched place. Ian and I pull out knives and, with frozen hands, scrape frozen logs until we have enough strips and chips to start a fire with the waterproof matches in his pack. As the bark kindling sputters into flame, George arrives. On foot. And with bad news.

He and his drivers have been looking for us for so long that they're low on gas. Very low. We'll have to ski out to the machines, which are parked another mile or so away. And one of them, the Argo, has thrown a bearing—it may or may not make it back down the mountain.

So before the struggling fire can warm us, we put on skis yet again and ski single file into the night. Guided only by moonlight, we lose our track once more. Then—finally—we come upon the waiting snow machines. We pile into the Argo. It groans, starts, and finally moves. At 4 miles an hour.

After a teeth-chattering ride through cold eternity, we at last reach George's Log Cabin Lodge. It's 11 P.M., pitch black, and we're in the early stages of hypothermia. We've been on the snow for twelve hours.

The lodge is blessedly warm. Within twenty minutes we've changed to dry clothes and are scoffing down a big dinner in front of the wood stove. Twenty minutes after we finish, we're huddling in bed, waiting for warmth and sleep to do their restorative work.

Winter's Diary: March 24

Morning Song. After several days of pushing through slush, I've finally switched from afternoon to morning skiing. What a difference! What a dummy for not trying it earlier!

The snow this morning is firm enough to keep me from sinking (except in a few sun-warmed hollows), yet soft enough to keep the skis from chattering on the downhills. I have plenty of glide, plenty of kick, and the morning sun on my shoulders. In short, it's a great time for cross-country skiing despite a thermometer reading of 50 degrees. Afterward, I spend fifteen minutes pulling the burdocks out of Sophie's coat. Every weed that sticks through the snow is a new adventure for her.

The skis no longer lean against the house with their tails in the snow. Now they lean against the house with their tails in the mud. Effin suggests it's time to put them away for the season, but I'm not ready to concede that this wonderful winter is really over. Although grass is showing around the houses, on the hilltops, and in ever-growing patches in the fields, I want to keep skiing. "Just one more day," I plead for the fourteenth time. She shakes her head in disbelief, but the skis stay outside.

That night, as we lay snuggled tight under quilts and blankets, Effin asked, "Did you really know we weren't going to die?"

"No. I just hoped so."

"Well, when you thought you might die, what were you thinking?"

I snuggled even tighter. "I thought how glad I was we'd made such beautiful love the night before."

"Oh, honey, that's nice."

"What were you thinking?"

Effin was silent a minute. Then I heard her chuckle. "Well . . . I thought how stupid it would be if I missed our daughters' high school graduation because I froze to death on a mountain in Newfoundland."

So what's to learn from all this? Here's what I got from the experience:

- *Never go high or far without a competent, well-equipped guide.* Both our guides carried maps and compasses. This proved fortunate when Ian's compass broke in the middle of the day. (The first rule of mountaineering is that when things start going wrong, they keep going wrong.) They also carried knives, walkie-talkies, extra food, extra clothes, a survival kit, a first-aid kit, a sleeping bag, and enough pots to boil water and dig a snow cave if we needed it. We almost needed it.

- *Never go high or far without proper gear and clothing.* Thankfully, most of our gear worked brilliantly. Our waxless Fischer Touring Crown skis had enough stability to grip on ice and enough glide to keep us from exhausting ourselves on snow. Effin and I both had the two essential accessories, hats and sunglasses. In the harsh sun on snowlight, I was glad I'd worn my wraparound Oakley Blades. I should have packed mittens; my Salomon gloves, though labeled "minus thirty," were made for racing, not mountaineering, and my fingers got cold as soon as the temperature dropped.

  We were wearing Duofold polyprop long johns under Nike ACG polyester pile. Both wicked perfectly. Over the pile, we wore Hind parkas and pants, which were good for keeping wind out but only fair at letting sweat out. When we lost the sun, Effin gained additional warmth by slipping a Canadian-made Far West Gore-Tex shell over her parka.

  But the prize of the day goes to our Salomon 711 (now model 811) cross-country ski boots. Their built-in cuffs kept our feet warm and dry while skiing, hiking, climbing, and even snowmobiling. They were comfortable, supportive, and the only thing I want to know is why I could not find a single pair for sale in the state of Vermont.

- *The visitor has a role too.* The guides' job was to shepherd us to safety, but we, too, had a job—in fact, two jobs: Stay cheerful, and stay out of the way.

  Whenever Dan or Ian asked how we were doing, feeling, or holding up, we always smiled and said, "Great!" When they were making decisions about what to do next, we discreetly withdrew. Just as well—I later learned that my increasingly fervent desire to head down into the gulch was typical of cold and tired skiers and hikers. They always want to go down rather than up, even when down—as in this case—can mean wandering around a densely forested ravine on a freezing night.

One final word on high-country skiing in Newfoundland: The months to go are March through May (through mid-June if you don't mind hiking to the snow). December, January, and February host too many sudden winter storms for safety. Early fishermen named the mountain range the Blow-Me-Downs. Remember that, and treat all Newfoundland high country with the respect it demands.

Winter's Diary: March 28

Conditional Surrender. The ground is practically bare. I know when I'm licked. I put the skis away. But just in case of an April snowstorm or a May blizzard, I leave the klister on their bottoms.

REFERENCES AND RESOURCES

BOOKS

Barnett, Steve. *Cross-Country Downhill.* 3rd ed. Seattle: Pacific Search Press, 1983.

A pioneer in backcountry downhill instruction. Originally published in 1978, it shows how telemarking and other downhill techniques can make the wilderness accessible in winter.

Bein, Vic. *Mountain Skiing.* Seattle: The Mountaineers, 1982.

Yes, it's dated, sometimes to the point of obsolescence. But if you find a copy at a used book sale, buy it anyway. The black and white photography is still unsurpassed in a backcountry ski book.

Borowski, Lee. *Basics of Modern Cross Country Skiing.* Lee W. Borowski (4500 Cherokee Dr., Brookfield, WI 53005), 1988.

Just thirty pages short, this is a primer for striding, skating, gear, and wax.

———. *The Simple Secrets of Skating.* Lee W. Borowski (4500 Cherokee Dr., Brookfield, WI 53005), 1986.

A booklet on skating technique meant to update Ski Faster, Easier.

———. *Ski Faster, Easier.* Human Kinetics Publishers (Sharon Kennedy, 800-747-4457, ext, 2288), 1986.

Coaching tips for everything from riding the glide ski to roller skiing (which gets a chapter on its own), all from a highly regarded competitor and coach.

Caldwell, John. *The New Cross-Country Ski Book.* 8th ed. Out of print but occasionally available on back shelves.

A crusty, opinionated, tough-guy-with-a-heart-of-gold book written by the three-time coach of the U.S. cross-country team. Covers history, personal stories, and Caldwell's training techniques, which include wood splitting, lawn mowing, and hiking from Canada to Massachusetts.

CCSAA. *The Best of Cross-Country Skiing.*

The Cross-Country Ski Areas Association (CCSAA) publishes an annual booklet that lists all its member areas. It costs under $5; call (603) 239-4341 with VISA or Mastercard in hand or write to CCSAA, 259 Bolton Rd., Winchester NH 03470. Fax (603) 239-6387, e-mail ccsaa@xcski.org, web site http://www.xcski.org.

Corcoran, Malcolm, *Waxing for Skiers.* Laval, Quebec: Guy Saint-Jean Éditeur, 1997.

If you want to get deeper into waxing, this is a straight-forward, no-theory, step-by-step how-to-it guide with 80 clear photos and illustrations to make it even plainer. Waxing for Skiers is available for C$16.95 from Guy Saint-Jean Éditeur, 674 Place Publique, bureau 200B, Laval, Quebec H7X 1G1 Canada. Their phone is (514) 689-6402. It's also available in French.

Endestad, Audun, and John Teaford. *Skating for Cross-Country Skiers.* Champaign, IL: Leisure Press, 1987.

A specialist guide to skating on skis. Major commitment to training, including weight training and schedule planning. Not for the casual skier.

Gillette, Ned, and John Dostal. *Cross-Country Skiing.* 3rd ed. The Mountaineers (1011 SW Klickitat Way, Seattle, WA 98134, 800-573-8484), 1988.

One of the most popular skinny-ski books of all time, probably because it's well written, useful, and fun. Besides giving solid technical advice, it tells tales of derring-do in high and scary places, near and far.

Gorman, Stephen. *AMC Guide to Winter Camping.* Boston: Appalachian Mountain Club, 1991,

A wilderness expert and successful journalist, Gorman tells you everything you need to know about winter camping, including a peek into snow caves and snow houses. Dress warm.

Gullion, Laurie. *The Cross Country Primer.* New York: Lyons & Burford, 1990.

Although ski technology has changed since this book was published, it's still a good beginner's guide.

———. *Nordic Skiing: Steps to Success.* Human Kinetics Publishers (800-747-4457), 1993.

If you're a step-by-step learner, this book's for you. It leads you through the fundamentals, one move at a time, from basic skills to accelerated skating.

———. Ski Games. Human Kinetics Publishers (800-747-4457), 1990.

Lessons from an accomplished instructor on teaching kids all kinds of skiing without whining or tears. For parents, instructors, and club leaders.

———. *Ski Games: A Fun-Filled Approach to Teaching Nordic and Alpine Skills.* Champaign, IL: Leisure Press, 1990.

Theoretically meant for kids, many of the games Gullion describes are excellent teaching aids for adults as well. So get ready for the Bobbing Stork, Bag of Bones, Power Slaps, and Pizza Tag.

LaChapelle, E. R. *The ABC of Avalanche Safety.* 2nd ed. Seattle: The Mountaineers, 1985.

This short book is a valuable resource for those who want to know more about avalanches, despite sentences like these: "Metamorphism within the snow cover is a continuous process which begins when the snow is deposited and continues until it melts. Destructive, or equitemperature (ET), metamorphism—the normal type—tends to destroy the original forms of deposited snow crystals, which are thereby gradually converted into rounded, isometric grains of ice."

Morton, John. *Don't Look Back.* Mechanicsburg, PA: Stackpole Books, 1992.

Good stuff—training and skiing pointers salted into a true tale of a forty-three year-old coach who, one fine day, decides to return to racing. What's more, Morton is not only a heck of a skier, he's a good storyteller as well.

Parker, Paul. *Free-Heel Skiing: The Comprehensive Guide to Downhill Ski Techniques for All Nordic Skiers.* 2nd ed. Seattle: The Mountaineers, 1995.

A little dated, but otherwise a honey of a book. Parker is a superb teacher and a damned good writer who tackles history, equipment, and especially, technique.

Powells, Brian. *Jack Rabbit—His First Hundred Years.* Ontario: Collier MacMillan, Ltd., 1975.

The definitive book about the founder of North American cross-country skiing, born June 15, 1875. The book was published on his hundredth birthday.

Swix. *Nordic Ski Preparation Tech Manual.* No date.

Short, information-packed, step-by-step waxing instruction. Seems to like products by Swix.

Tokle, Art, and Martin Luray. *The Complete Guide to Cross-Country Skiing & Touring*. Revised edition. New York: Vintage Books, 1977.

Everything in this book is outdated everything—except the writing. Along with advice on wooden skis with mohair bases, it contains some of the sweetest descriptions of backcountry skiing ever put to paper.

Toko AG. *Wax Book*. Switzerland, No date.

A short, useful guide to waxing for nordic, alpine, and snowboard.

Townsend, Chris. *Wilderness Skiing and Winter Camping*. Camden, ME: Ragged Mountain Press, 1994.

A backcountry guide that includes chapters on load carrying, living in the snow, and a ski tour in the Canadian Rockies.

Wilkerson, James, ed. *Medicine for Mountaineering*. 4th ed. The Mountaineers (1011 SW Klickitat Way, Seattle, WA 98134, 800-573-8484), 1992.

Williams, Knox, and Betsy Armstrong. *The Snowy Torrents: Avalanche Accidents in the United States 1972-79*. Jackson, WY: Teton Bookshop Publishing, no date.

An absolutely macabre book, yet one that is as potentially useful as it is morbidly fascinating. The book is nothing more than a compilation of 145 avalanche accident reports, some accompanied by maps and photos. Here's a sample conclusion: "Despite a textbook rescue effort. . . the victim died. The warning is clear: the chances of recovery from an avalanche burial should always be considered slim."

TOURING GUIDES

Bushey, Steve. *Vermont Cross-Country Ski Atlas*. Burlington, VT: Northern Cartographic, 1983.

It's getting a bit dated, but this guide to ski-touring centers in the Green Mountains rates them, trail by trail, according to difficulty.

Conroy, Dennis, and Shirley Matzke. *Adirondack Cross-Country Skiing*. Woodstock, VT: Backcountry Publications, 1992.

A detailed guide to seventy trails through the Adirondack Mountains of New York State.

DuMais, Richard. *50 Ski Tours in Jackson Hole and Yellowstone.* Boulder, CO: High Peak Books, 1990.

Ski past bison, mud pools, geysers, and some of the most photographed scenery in North America. The tours range from flat and easy to precipitous and extremely challenging. Either way, dress warmly.

Elman, Raymond. *A Critical Guide to Cross Country Ski Areas: The Best of New England's Touring Centers.* Lexington, MA: Stephen Greene Press, 1987. *Out of print.*

Fitzgerald, John R. *Cross Country Northeast: A Guide to the Best Cross Country Skiing Areas and Inns of New England and New York.* La Crescenta, CA: Mountain Air Books, 1994.

Goodman, David. *Classic Backcountry Skiing: A Guide to the Best Ski Tours in New England.* Boston: Appalachian Mountain Club, 1989.

This has already become something of a skiing classic and winner of a North American ski writing award. Goodman "encourages skiers to return once again to the high and wild places of New England" by revealing the location, elevation, and degree of difficulty of ski trails, many of them long forgotten, throughout the region. Expect a new and expanded edition in fall of 1998.

Kirkendall, Tom, and V. Spring. *Cross Country Ski Tours. Washington's North Cascades.* 2nd ed. Seattle: The Mountaineers, 1996.

More than eighty backcountry tours with 64 maps.

———. *Washington's South Cascades & Olympics.* 2nd ed. Seattle: The Mountaineers, 1995.

Lamy, Marge. *Cross Country Ski Inns: Northeastern U.S. & Quebec.* East Haven, CT: Inland Book Co., 1991.

Describes thirty-seven distinguished ski inns from Pennsylvania to Quebec.

Leggett, Christopher, and Woden Teachout. *Tracks & Trails: An Insider's Guide to the Best Cross Country Skiing in the Northeast.* Duxbury, MA: Dawbert Press, 1995.

Litz, Brian, and Kurt Lankford. *Skiing Colorado's Backcountry.* Golden, CO: Fulcrum, 1989.

Well above the average ski guide, this book gives interesting history and local lore as well as trail maps and elevations. Nice black and white photos, too.

McGrath, William Chad. *Stride and Glide: A Guide to Wisconsin's Best Cross-Country Ski Trails*. Schofield, WI: ClearView Books, 1994.

Olsen, Ken, Dena Olsen, Steve and Hazel Scharosch. *Cross Country Skiing Yellowstone Country*. Casper, WY: Abacus Enterprises, 1992.

Schweiker, Roioli. *25 Ski Tours in New Hampshire*. Woodstock, VT: Countryman Press (Helen Whybrow, 800-245-4151), 1988.

From the White Mountains to the Atlantic Ocean, you can ski your way through the Live Free or Die state. Out of print.

Seguin, Yves. *Ski de fond au Quebec*. Montreal, Canada: Editions Ulysses, 1994.

Terrell, Mike. *Northern Michigan's Best Cross-Country Ski Trails in the Lower Peninsula*. Williamsburg, MI: Outdoor Recreational Press, 1995.

Solid advice from the man who knows the Peninsula best.

Vielbig, Klindt. *Cross-Country Ski Routes: Oregon*. 2nd ed. Seattle: The Mountaineers, 1994.

Five hundred trails covering 2,000 miles in Oregon and southwest Washington.

Wiesel, Jonathan. *Cross-Country Ski Vacations*. Santa Fe, NM: John Muir Publications, 1997.

This is the book I've longed for. It's a learned, literate, humorous, opinionated guide to the best cross-country ski resorts, centers, and trail systems in North America. Looking for an area with moderate prices, night skiing, and romantic ambience, that has horse-drawn sleigh rides and an airport within 50 miles? Wiesel's book will find it for you. Don't leave home without it!

MAGAZINES

Back Country. 7065 Dover Way, Arvada, CO 80004, (303) 424-5858.

Dedicated to the full range of backcountry skiing, from ski mountaineering to touring on rolling terrain.

Couloir. P.O.B. 2349, Truckee, CA 96160, (916) 582-1884, couloir@telis.org, www.couloir-mag.com.

A couloir is a steep, narrow mountainside chute. "Earn your turns" is Couloir's *motto. That translates into a mag of extremes. No beginner's slopes or touring centers here—it's hell for leather, high-mountain adventure all the way.*

Cross Country Skier. 1823 Fremont Ave. S., Minneapolis, MN 55403, (612) 377-0312, http://www.crosscountryskier.com.

The granddaddy of skinny-ski mags, with articles for beginners and experts, on health and equipment, covering locales east and west.

Outside. P.O.B. 51733, Boulder, CO 80323-1733, (800) 678-1131.

An elegantly written magazine about the outdoors, Outside *is a literary treat, the* New Yorker *with an ice ax. It frequently features articles about ski adventure and equipment.*

Powder. P.O. Box 58144, Boulder, CO 80323-8144.

True, Powder *is mainly an alpine ski magazine, but when it covers the backcountry, it does a bang-up job.*

Silent Sports. P.O. Box 152, Waupaca, WI 54981, (715) 258-5546.

The magazine of engineless recreational activity.

Ski Trax. 2 Pardee Ave., Suite 204, Toronto M6K 3H5, (416) 530-1350, e-mail skitrax@passport.ca.

Cross-country from racing to track skiing to backcountry in Canada and the United States.

VIDEOS

Avalanche Awareness. Alliance Communications, 1988.

Grimly matter-of-fact and all too real. If you need a reminder of how deadly avalanches can be, watch this tape.

Beyond the Groomed: Free Heel Skiing Off-Piste. Nils Larsen (Free Heels, P.O. Box 117, Curlew, WA 99118, 509-779-4674), 1996.

A first video from backcountry expert Nils Larsen. Beautiful shooting, unusually fine soundtrack, and instruction that's only comprehensible to viewers conversant with telebonics. For the rest of us, it offers thirty-four minutes of inspiration but not much in the way of usable instruction.

Revenge of the Telemarkers. North American Telemark Organization, 1989.

Takes up where The Telemark Movie *leaves off. Plenty of shots and tips on skiing steeps, moguls, and other scary stuff.*

The Simple Secrets of Skating. Lee Borowski, 1987.
Though a bit dated, it's a good way to see the basics of ski-skating and learn them from an expert.

Skiing the Wild Snow. Glenn Vitucci, 1995.
Some good tips but not a lot else. A lot of talking, some questionable technique, and next to nothing on skiing downhill.

The Telemark Movie. North American Telemark Organization, 1987.
Learn the turn, one step at a time. Plenty of stop-action and slow-motion sequences to make the learning painless.

The Telemark Workshop. North American Telemark Organization, 1992.
More telemark turn lessons. Includes jump turns, uphill skiing, and self-arrest on the ultrasteeps.

CATALOGS

Akers Ski, One Akers Way, Andover, ME 04216-0280, (207) 392-4582, www.megalink.net/~akers.
In addition to name-brand products, Akers sells closeouts, irregulars, and special values.

Backcountry Bookstore, P.O. Box 6235, Lynnwood, WA 98036-0235, (206) 290-7652, fax (206) 290 9461.
A major distributor of outdoor books and videos.

Black Diamond Equipment, 2084 E. 3900 S., Salt Lake City, UT 84124, (801) 278-5553.
Replete with gorgeous photography, Black Diamond's catalog offers skis and boots, bindings and poles, crampons and ice axes, and more.

Eagle River Nordic, (800) 423-9730, www.ernordic.com.
A catalog of high-performance ski gear, computer selected and guaranteed to fit.

Early Winters, (800) 458-4438.
Cold-weather gear from ski pants to snowshoes.

Lands' End, One Lands' End Lane, Dodgeville, WI 53595, (800) 356-4444.
Lands' End winter catalog carries a broad range of outdoor activewear.

L. L. Bean, Freeport, ME 04033, (800) 341-4341.
Best known for clothing, L. L. Bean also carries a wide range of skis, boots, and accessories ranging from Swiss army knives to climbing skins.

New Moon Ski Shop Catalog, P.O. Box 591, Highway 63N, Hayward, WI 54843, (800) 754-8685.
Tell them your needs, and they'll send you the right skis, poles, underwear, the works—and guaranteed to fit! More than two decades of experience.

Nordic Equipment Inc., P.O. Box 997, Park City, UT 84060, (800) 321-1671, fax (801) 649-2994.
Owned by award-winning coach Tobjorn Karlsen and run by nordic specialists. Sells ski gear and limited skiwear.

Reliable Racing Nordic Sports Catalog, (800) 517-7555, Sarah Mannix, PR, (800) 223-4448, ext. 230.
Long a major player in alpine sports, Reliable Racing has entered the nordic field with a full-color thirty-two-page catalog filled with Norwegian sweaters, tuning supplies, roller skis, and more.

Sierra Nordic, 21455 Donner Pass Rd., P.O. Box 905, Soda Springs, CA 95728, orders (800) 426-4566, questions (916) 426-9165, fax (916) 426-0922.
Sierra Nordic is a specialized cross-country ski store with a nationwide mail-order service. Big Labor Day sale (even the sales show up in the minicatalogs).

Ski & Snowbound Tools, Tögner Toolworks, (800) 299-9904 or (916) 926-2600, fax (800) 926-9904.
A witty, opinionated, useful, and thoroughly delightful catalog printed on recycled paper and containing everything from aprons to drip candles, slopemeters to wax irons. Tögner is tops in tuning.

MAJOR MANUFACTURERS

Skis: Alpina, Atomic, Black Diamond, Blizzard, Exel, Fischer, Garmont, Karhu, Kazama, Madshus, Rossignol, Trak, Tua, Yostmark.

Boots: Alico, Alpina, Black Diamond, Erik Sports, Exel, Garmont, Jarvinen, Karhu, Merrell, Nordica, Rossignol, Salomon, San Marco, Tecnica.

Bindings: Rottefella, Salomon.

Poles: Action Sports, Alpina, Back Country Access, Black Diamond, CEBE, Excel, Goode, Leki, Life-Link, Ramer, Swix.

Wax: Briko, Rex, Rode, Solda, Start, Swix, Toko.

ORGANIZATIONS

Canadian Ski Council, (905) 677-0020, fax (905) 677-2055, www.skicanada.org.

Catamount Trail Association, P.O. Box 1235, Burlington, VT 05402, (802) 864-5794, http://twilight.vsc.edu/~pchapin/cta.

A nonprofit organization devoted to developing and managing the 280-mile Catamount Trail, "The Length of Vermont on Skis."

Cross-Country Ski Areas Association, 259 Bolton Rd., Winchester, NH 03470, (603) 239-4341.

Promotes its many member cross-country ski areas across North America.

North American Telemark Organization (NATO), Box 44, Waitsfield, VT 05673, (800) 835-3404 or (802) 496-4387.

"The world's oldest and largest Telemark and Backcountry skiing promotional and educational resource." NATO runs courses, clinics, camps, and adventure tours and makes telemark videos.